To

_____

From

_____

Date

_____

PROMISES & PRAYERS

for
Teachers

SECOND EDITION

PROMISES *&* PRAYERS

for
Teachers

FAMILY CHRISTIAN PRESS
Grand Rapids, MI 49530

The quoted ideas expressed in this book (but not scripture verses) are not, in all cases, exact quotations, as some have been edited for clarity and brevity. In all cases, the author has attempted to maintain the speaker's original intent. In some cases, quoted material for this book was obtained from secondary sources, primarily print media. While every effort was made to ensure the accuracy of these sources, the accuracy cannot be guaranteed. For additions, deletions, corrections or clarifications in future editions of this text, please write FAMILY CHRISTIAN PRESS.

Scripture quotations are taken from:

The Holy Bible, King James Version

The Holy Bible, New International Version (NIV) Copyright © 1973, 1978, 1984, by International Bible Society. Used by permission of Zondervan Publishing House. All rights reserved.

The Holy Bible, New King James Version (NKJV) Copyright © 1982 by Thomas Nelson, Inc. Used by permission.

The New American Standard Bible®, (NASB) Copyright © 1960, 1962, 1963, 1968, 1971, 1972, 1973, 1975, 1977, 1995 by The Lockman Foundation. Used by permission.

Holy Bible, New Living Translation, (NLT) Copyright © 1996. Used by permission of Tyndale House Publishers, Inc., Wheaton, Illinois 60189. All rights reserved.

New Century Version®. (NCV) Copyright © 1987, 1988, 1991 by Word Publishing, a division of Thomas Nelson, Inc. All rights reserved. Used by permission.

The Message (MSG)- This edition issued by contractual arrangement with NavPress, a division of The Navigators, U.S.A. Originally published by NavPress in English as THE MESSAGE: The Bible in Contemporary Language copyright 2002-2003 by Eugene Peterson. All rights reserved.

Revised Standard Version. (RSV) Copyright © 1946, 1952, 1959, 1973 by the Division of Christian Education of the National Council of the Churches of Christ in the United States of America. All rights reserved. Used by permission.

The Holman Christian Standard Bible™ (HCSB) Copyright © 1999, 2000, 2001 by Holman Bible Publishers. Used by permission.

International Children's Bible®, New Century Version®. (ICB) Copyright © 1986, 1988, 1999 by Tommy Nelson™, a division of Thomas Nelson, Inc. All rights reserved. Used by permission.

Cover Design by Kim Russell / Wahoo Designs
Page Layout by Bart Dawson

ISBN 1-58334-237-0

Printed in the United States of America

FAMILY
CHRISTIAN
PRESS

Table of Contents

Introduction

If you're a teacher, please accept hearty congratulations and a profound word of thanks. Henry Adams was correct when he observed, "A teacher affects eternity; he can never tell where his influence stops." And never have those words been more true than they are today. We live in a difficult age, an age of unparalleled distractions and temptations. During these trying times, our young people need the direction and the leadership that comes from teachers who know and love God.

This book is intended for Christians who teach. Each brief chapter contains Bible verses, a quotation from a noted thinker, and a prayer. These pages provide helpful reminders for the modern-day challenges that face teachers and students alike.

Whether you teach graduate school or Sunday School, whether you lecture at seminary or at Vacation Bible School, you need and deserve a regularly scheduled conference with the Ultimate Teacher. After all, you are God's emissary, a person charged with molding lives—a truly awesome responsibility. God takes your teaching duties very seriously, and so should you.

So, take the time to carefully consider the promises and prayers on these pages. And as you do so, remember that God honors your profession just as surely as He offers

His loving abundance to you and your students. With God's help, you, in your role as a concerned teacher, are destined to reshape eternity. It's a big job, but don't worry; together, you and God can handle it.

Abundance

I have come that they may have life,
and that they may have it more abundantly.

John 10:10 NKJV

His master replied, "Well done, good and faithful servant!
You have been faithful with a few things;
I will put you in charge of many things.
Come and share your master's happiness!"

Matthew 25:21 NIV

My cup runs over. Surely goodness and mercy
shall follow me all the days of my life;
And I will dwell in the house of the Lord forever.

Psalm 23:5, 6 NKJV

Now this I say, he who sows sparingly
will also reap sparingly, and he who sows bountifully
will also reap bountifully.

2 Corinthians 9:6 NASB

Commit to the Lord whatever you do,
and your plans will succeed.

Proverbs 16:3 NIV

The 10th chapter of John reminds us of the abundance that can be ours through Christ. But what, exactly, did Jesus mean when He promised "life . . . more abundantly?" Was He referring to material possessions or financial wealth? Hardly. Jesus offers a different kind of abundance: a spiritual richness that extends beyond the temporal boundaries of this world. This everlasting abundance is available to all who seek it and claim it. May we, as believers, claim the riches of Christ Jesus every day that we live, and may we share His blessings with our students, with our families, with our coworkers, and with the world.

Instead of living a black-and-white existence,
we'll be released into a Technicolor world of vibrancy
and emotion when we more accurately reflect
His nature to the world around us.

Bill Hybels

— A Prayer —

Heavenly Father, You have promised an abundant life
through Your Son Jesus. Thank You, Lord, for
Your abundance. Guide me according to Your will,
so that I might be a worthy teacher in all
that I say and do, this day and every day.

Amen

Anger

*I want men everywhere to lift up holy hands in prayer,
without anger or disputing.*

1 Timothy 2:8 NIV

*Now you must rid yourselves of all such things as these:
anger, rage, malice . . . .*

Colossians 3:8 NIV

Don't become angry quickly, because getting angry is foolish.

Ecclesiastes 7:9 NCV

*But I tell you that men will have to give account on
the day of judgment for every careless word
they have spoken. For by your words you will be
acquitted, and by your words you will be condemned.*

Matthew 12:36, 37 NIV

*A patient man has great understanding,
but a quick-tempered man displays folly.*

Proverbs 14:29 NIV

Teaching, like every job, has its fair share of frustrations—some great, and some small. Sometimes, those frustrations may cause you to reach the boiling point. But here's a word of warning: When you're tempted to lose your temper over the minor inconveniences of the teaching profession, don't do it—don't give voice to your angry thoughts.

If you make haste to speak angry words, you will inevitably say things that you'll soon regret. Remember: God will help you control your temper *if* you ask Him to do so. And the time to ask Him is *before* your temper gets the best of you—not after.

Anger breeds remorse in the heart,
discord in the home, bitterness in the community,
and confusion in the state.

Billy Graham

— A Prayer —

Lord, I can be so impatient, and I can become so angry.
Calm me down, Lord, and give me the maturity and
the wisdom to be a patient, forgiving teacher. Just as
You have forgiven me, Father, let me forgive others so
that I can follow the example of Your Son.

Amen

Anxiety

Cast all your anxiety on him because he cares for you.
1 Peter 5:7 NIV

*Peace I leave with you, my peace I give unto you:
not as the world giveth, give I unto you.
Let not your heart be troubled, neither let it be afraid.*
John 14:27 KJV

*Come to me, all you who are weary and burdened,
and I will give you rest. Take my yoke upon you
and learn from me, for I am gentle and humble in heart,
and you will find rest for your souls.
For my yoke is easy and my burden is light.*
Matthew 11:28-30 NIV

*Therefore I tell you, do not worry about your life,
what you will eat or drink; or about your body,
what you will wear. Is not life more important than food,
and the body more important than clothes? Look at the birds
of the air; they do not sow or reap or store away in barns,
and yet your heavenly Father feeds them.
Are you not much more valuable than they?*
Matthew 6:25-27 NIV

Because we are imperfect human beings, we worry. Even though we are Christians who have been given the assurance of salvation—even though we are Christians who have received the promise of God's love and protection—we find ourselves fretting over the countless details of everyday life. Jesus understood our concerns when He spoke the reassuring words found in Matthew 6: "Therefore I tell you, do not worry about your life . . ."

As you consider the promises of Jesus, remember that God still sits in His heaven and you are His beloved child. Then, perhaps, you will worry a little less and trust God a little more, and that's as it should be because God is trustworthy . . . and you are protected.

The beginning of anxiety is the end of faith, and
the beginning of true faith is the end of anxiety.

George Mueller

— A Prayer —

Lord, sometimes this world is a difficult place, and,
as a frail human being, I am fearful. When I am
worried, restore my faith. When I am anxious, turn my
thoughts to You. When I grieve, touch my heart with
Your enduring love. And, keep me mindful, Lord, that
nothing, absolutely nothing, will happen this day that
You and I cannot handle together.

Amen

Asking God

*So I say to you, ask, and it will be given to you; seek,
and you will find; knock, and it will be opened to you.
For everyone who asks receives, and he who seeks finds,
and to him who knocks it will be opened.*

Luke 11:9, 10 NKJV

*You did not choose me, but I chose you and appointed you
to go and bear fruit—fruit that will last.
Then the Father will give you whatever you ask in my name.*

John 15:16 NIV

You do not have, because you do not ask God.

James 4:2 NIV

*Verily, verily, I say unto you, He that believeth on me,
the works that I do shall he do also; and greater works than
these shall he do; because I go unto my Father.
And whatsoever ye shall ask in my name, that will I do,
that the Father may be glorified in the Son.
If ye shall ask any thing in my name, I will do it.*

John 14:12-14 KJV

God gives the gifts; we, as believers, should accept them—but oftentimes, we don't. Why? Because we fail to trust our Heavenly Father completely, and because we are, at times, surprisingly stubborn. Luke 11 teaches us that God does not withhold spiritual gifts from those who ask. Our obligation, quite simply, is to ask.

Are you asking God to move mountains in your life, or are you expecting Him to stumble over molehills? Whatever the size of your challenges, God is big enough to handle them. Ask for His help today, with faith and with fervor, and then watch in amazement as your mountains begin to move.

> We honor God by asking for great things when they are a part of His promise. We dishonor Him and cheat ourselves when we ask for molehills where He has promised mountains.
>
> *Vance Havner*

— A Prayer —

Lord, when I have questions or fears, let me turn to You. When I am weak, let me seek Your strength. When I am discouraged, Father, keep me mindful of Your love and Your grace. In all things, let me seek Your will and Your way, Dear Lord, today and forever.

Amen

Attitude

*Your attitude should be the same as that of Christ Jesus:
Who, being in very nature God, did not consider equality
with God something to be grasped, but made himself nothing,
taking the very nature of a servant, being made in human
likeness. And being found in appearance as a man,
he humbled himself and became obedient to death—
even death on a cross!*

Philippians 2:5-8 NIV

*You were taught, with regard to your former way of life,
to put off your old self, which is being corrupted by its
deceitful desires; to be made new in the attitude of
your minds; and to put on the new self,
created to be like God in true righteousness and holiness.*

Ephesians 4:22-24 NIV

*A miserable heart means a miserable life;
a cheerful heart fills the day with a song.*

Proverbs 15:15 MSG

*For the word of God is living and active.
Sharper than any double-edged sword, it penetrates
even to dividing soul and spirit, joints and marrow;
it judges the thoughts and attitudes of the heart.*

Hebrews 4:12 NIV

As the leader of your classroom, you must beware: your attitudes are contagious. If you're upbeat and optimistic, your students will tend to emulate you. But, if you fall prey to cynicism or pessimism, many of your students will, too. How will you direct your thoughts today? Will you obey the words of Philippians 4:8 by dwelling upon those things that are pure, lovely, and admirable? Or will you allow your thoughts to be hijacked by the negativity that seems to dominate our troubled world?

God intends that you experience joy and abundance, but He will not force His joy upon you; you must claim it for yourself. So, today and every day hereafter, focus your thoughts and your energies upon "things that are excellent and worthy of praise." When you celebrate life, you'll soon discover that many of your students will join in the celebration.

I could go through this day oblivious to the miracles
all around me, or I could tune in and "enjoy."

Gloria Gaither

— A Prayer —

Dear Lord, let me live my life and love my students with
a spirit of optimism and hope. Whatever circumstances
I face, whether good or bad, triumphal or tragic,
may my response reflect a God-honoring,
Christlike attitude of faith and love for You.

Amen

Celebration

*David and the whole house of Israel were celebrating
with all their might before the LORD, with songs
and with harps, lyres, tambourines, sistrums and cymbals.*

2 Samuel 6:5 NIV

Celebrate God all day, every day. I mean, revel in him!

Philippians 4:4 MSG

*Delight thyself also in the LORD;
and he shall give thee the desires of thine heart.*

Psalm 37:4 KJV

*Shout for joy to the LORD, all the earth.
Worship the LORD with gladness;
come before him with joyful songs.*

Psalm 100:1, 2 NIV

*This is the day the LORD has made.
We will rejoice and be glad in it.*

Psalm 118:24 NLT

Are you a teacher who celebrates life? Hopefully you are! God has richly blessed you, and He wants you to rejoice in His gifts.

The 118th Psalm reminds us that today, like every other day, is a cause for celebration. God gives us this day; He fills it to the brim with possibilities, and He challenges us to use it for His purposes. Today is a non-renewable resource—once it's gone, it's gone forever. Our responsibility—as Christians and as teachers— is to use this day in the service of God's will as we share His wisdom and His love.

> A child of God should be a visible beatitude for joy and a living doxology for gratitude.
>
> *C. H. Spurgeon*

— A Prayer —

Dear Lord, You have given me so many reasons to celebrate. Today, let me choose an attitude of cheerfulness. Let me be a joyful Christian, Lord, quick to laugh and slow to anger. And, let me share Your goodness with my family, my friends, my neighbors, and my students, this day and every day.

Amen

Children

I have no greater joy than this,
to hear of my children walking in the truth.

3 John 1:4 NASB

I assure you: Whoever does not welcome
the kingdom of God like a little child will never enter it.

Luke 18:17 HCSB

Even a child is known by his actions,
by whether his conduct is pure and right.

Proverbs 20:11 NIV

Train a child in the way he should go,
and when he is old he will not turn from it.

Proverbs 22:6 NIV

Suffer the little children to come unto me,
and forbid them not; for of such is the kingdom of God.
Verily I say unto you, Whosoever shall not receive
the kingdom of God as a little child, he shall not
enter therein. And he took them up in his arms,
put his hands upon them, and blessed them.

Mark 10:14-16 KJV

Every child is unique, but every child is similar in this respect: He or she is a priceless gift from God—and with that gift comes immense responsibilities for parents and teachers alike.

Even during those strenuous days when the classroom is in an uproar and the papers are piled to the ceiling, wise teachers never forget the overriding goal of their profession: shaping young minds. The very best teachers shape those minds with love, with discipline, and with God.

Every child born into the world is a new thought of God, an ever-fresh and radiant possibility.

Kate Douglas Wiggin

— A Prayer —

Thank You, Lord, for the priceless gift of children.
Let me always be mindful of the profound
responsibilities of teaching, and let me teach
my students to know You and to walk with You always.
Amen

Conscience

For God is pleased with you when, for the sake of your conscience, you patiently endure unfair treatment.

1 Peter 2:19 NLT

So I strive always to keep my conscience clear before God and man.

Acts 24:16 NIV

. . . they show that the requirements of the law are written on their hearts, their consciences also bearing witness, and their thoughts now accusing, now even defending them.

Romans 2:15 NIV

Let us draw near to God with a sincere heart in full assurance of faith, having our hearts sprinkled to cleanse us from a guilty conscience and having our bodies washed with pure water.

Hebrews 10:22 NIV

Do not conform any longer to the pattern of this world, but be transformed by the renewing of your mind. Then you will be able to test and approve what God's will is—his good, pleasing and perfect will.

Romans 12:2 NIV

S imply put, a guilty conscience has the power to torment us. And thankfully, the opposite is also true: Few things in life provide more contentment than a clear conscience—a clear conscience that results from the knowledge that we are obeying God's commandments.

Thoughtful teachers (like you) understand the importance of wise choices and the rewards of a clear conscience . . . and thoughtful teachers (like you) share that message with their students.

The beginning of backsliding means your conscience does not answer to the truth.

Oswald Sanders

— A Prayer —

Dear Lord, You speak to me through the Bible, through the words of others, and through that still, small voice within. Through my conscience, You reveal Your will for my life. Show me Your plan for this day, Heavenly Father, and let me share the Good News of Your Son.

Amen

Courage

Be strong and courageous, and do the work.
Don't be afraid or discouraged by the size of the task,
for the LORD God, my God, is with you.
He will not fail you or forsake you.

1 Chronicles 28:20 NLT

Be strong and courageous. Do not be terrified;
do not be discouraged, for the LORD your God
will be with you wherever you go.

Joshua 1:9 NIV

The LORD himself goes before you and will be with you;
he will never leave you nor forsake you. Do not be afraid;
do not be discouraged.

Deuteronomy 31:8 NIV

I can do everything through him that gives me strength.

Philippians 4:13 NIV

So do not fear, for I am with you; do not be dismayed,
for I am your God. I will strengthen you and help you;
I will uphold you with my righteous right hand.

Isaiah 41:10 NIV

Every human life, like every teaching career, is a tapestry of events: some grand, some not-so-grand, and some heartbreaking. When we reach the mountaintops of life, praising God is easy. But, when the storm clouds form overhead and we find ourselves in the dark valley of life, our faith is stretched, sometimes to the breaking point.

As believers, we can be comforted: Wherever we find ourselves, whether at the top of the mountain or the depths of the valley, God is there, and because He cares for us, we can live courageously.

The fear of God is the death of every other fear.

C. H. Spurgeon

— A Prayer —

Lord, at times, this world is a fearful place.
At times, I fear for my family and for my students.
Yet, You have promised that You are with me always.
With You as my protector, I am not afraid.
Today, Dear Lord, let me live courageously
as I place my trust in You.
Amen

Encouraging Others

Finally, all of you should be of one mind,
full of sympathy toward each other, loving one another
with tender hearts and humble minds.

1 Peter 3:8 NLT

Encourage each other. Live in harmony and peace.
Then the God of love and peace will be with you.

2 Corinthians 13:11 NLT

Let the word of Christ dwell in you richly in all wisdom;
teaching and admonishing one another in psalms and
hymns and spiritual songs, singing with
grace in your hearts to the Lord.

Colossians 3:16 KJV

Let us consider how to stimulate one another
to love and good deeds.

Hebrews 10:24 NASB

Watch the way you talk. Let nothing foul or dirty
come out of your mouth. Say only what helps,
each word a gift.

Ephesians 4:29 MSG

For young people experiencing life here in the new Millennium, the world can be a difficult and uncertain place. Many of our students are in desperate need of a smile or an encouraging word, and since we don't always know who needs our help, the best strategy is to encourage all those who cross our paths.

Life is a team sport, and all of us need occasional pats on the back from our teammates and our coaches. Great teachers, like great coaches, inspire their students to learn, to work, to grow, and to persevere. And never has the need been greater for teachers who understand the art of encouragement.

To the loved, a word of affection is a morsel, but
to the love-starved, a word of affection can be a feast.

Max Lucado

— A Prayer —

Dear Father, make me an encouraging teacher.
Just as You have lifted me up, let me also lift up
my students in the spirit of encouragement and hope.
Today, let me help my students find the strength and
the courage to use their gifts according
to Your master plan.
Amen

Enthusiasm

Do your work with enthusiasm.
Work as if you were serving the Lord,
not as if you were serving only men and women.

Ephesians 6:7 NCV

Never be lacking in zeal, but keep your spiritual fervor,
serving the Lord.

Romans 12:11 NIV

Those who hope in the LORD will renew their strength. They
will soar on wings like eagles; they will run and
not grow weary, they will walk and not be faint.

Isaiah 40:31 NIV

The plans of the diligent lead to profit.

Proverbs 21:5 NIV

He did it with all his heart, and prospered.

2 Chronicles 31:21 KJV

Norman Vincent Peale advised, "Get absolutely enthralled with something. Throw yourself into it with abandon. Get out of yourself. Be somebody. Do something." His words still ring true, especially in the classroom. But sometimes, when the stresses of everyday life seem overwhelming, you may not feel very enthusiastic about yourself *or* your students.

If you're a teacher with too many obligations and too few hours in which to meet them, you are not alone. Teaching can be a demanding profession. But don't fret. Instead, focus upon God and upon His love for you. Then, ask Him for the strength you need to fulfill your responsibilities. God will give you the enthusiasm to do the most important things on today's to-do list . . . if you ask Him. So ask Him. Now.

Wherever you are, be all there. Live to the hilt every situation you believe to be the will of God.

Jim Elliot

— A Prayer —

Lord, when the classroom leaves me exhausted,
let me turn to You for strength and for renewal.
When I follow Your will for my life, You will renew
my enthusiasm. Let Your will be my will, Lord,
and let me find my strength in You.

Amen

Example

In everything set them an example by doing what is good.

Titus 2:7 NIV

You are the light that gives light to the world.
In the same way, you should be a light for other people.
Live so that they will see the good things you do and
will praise your Father in heaven.

Matthew 5:14, 16 NCV

Be an example to the believers in word, in conduct,
in love, in spirit, in faith, in purity.

1 Timothy 4:12 NKJV

You shall walk in all the way which the Lord your God
has commanded you, that you may live, and that it may be
well with you, and that you may prolong your days in
the land which you will possess.

Deuteronomy 5:33 NASB

He will teach us of his ways, and we will walk in his paths.

Isaiah 2:3 KJV

We teach our students by the words we speak and the lives we lead, but not necessarily in that order. Sometimes, our actions speak so loudly that they drown out our words completely. That's why, as teachers, we must make certain that the lives we lead are in harmony with the lessons we preach.

Are you the kind of teacher whose life serves as a memorable model of righteousness and godliness? If so, you are a powerful force for good in your classroom and in your world.

Phillips Brooks advised, "Be such a man, and live such a life, that if every man were such as you, and every life a life like yours, this earth would be God's Paradise." And that's sound advice because our families and our students are watching . . . and so, for that matter, is God.

More depends on my walk than my talk.
D. L. Moody

— A Prayer —

Dear Lord, because I am a teacher, I am an example
to my students. Let me be a worthy example,
Father, so that my words and my deeds
may be a tribute to You.
Amen

Faith

We live by faith, not by sight.

2 Corinthians 5:7 NIV

Have faith in the LORD *your God and you will be upheld.*

2 Chronicles 20:20 NIV

The fundamental fact of existence is that this trust in God,
this faith, is the firm foundation under everything
that makes life worth living.

Hebrews 11:1 MSG

But without faith it is impossible to please him:
for he that cometh to God must believe that he is,
and that he is a rewarder of them that diligently seek him.

Hebrews 11:6 KJV

Faith without works is dead . . . .

James 2:20 KJV

Have you ever felt your faith in God slipping away? If so, you are not alone. Every life—including yours—is a series of successes and failures, celebrations and disappointments, joys and sorrows. But even when we feel very distant from God, God is never distant from us.

Jesus taught His disciples that if they had faith, they could move mountains. You can too. When you place your faith, your trust, indeed your life in the hands of Christ Jesus, you'll be amazed at the marvelous things He can do with you and through you. So strengthen your faith through praise, through worship, through Bible study, and through prayer. And trust God's plans. With Him, all things are possible, and He stands ready to open a world of possibilities to you *if* you have faith.

I do beg of you to recognize the extreme simplicity of faith; it is nothing more nor less than just believing God when He says He either has done something for us, or will do it; and then trusting Him to do it. It is so simple that it is hard to explain.

Hannah Whitall Smith

— A Prayer —

Dear Lord, help me to be a teacher whose faith is strong and whose heart is pure. Help me to remember that You are always near and that You can overcome any challenge. With Your love and Your power, Lord, I can live courageously and faithfully today and every day.
Amen

Forgiveness

Then Peter came to him and asked,
"Lord, how often should I forgive
someone who sins against me? Seven times?"
"No!" Jesus replied, "seventy times seven!"
Matthew 18:21, 22 NLT

Why do you look at the speck of sawdust in your brother's
eye and pay no attention to the plank in your own eye?
How can you say to your brother, "Let me take the speck
out of your eye," when all the time there is a plank in
your own eye? You hypocrite, first take the plank out of
your own eye, and then you will see clearly to remove
the speck from your brother's eye.
Matthew 7:3-5 NIV

For if you forgive men when they sin against you,
your heavenly Father will also forgive you.
But if you do not forgive men their sins,
your Father will not forgive your sins.
Matthew 6:14, 15 NIV

And be kind and compassionate to one another,
forgiving one another, just as God also forgave you in Christ.
Ephesians 4:32 HCSB

As believers, we are commanded to forgive others, just as God has forgiven us. But oftentimes, we find it quite difficult to forgive the people who have hurt us badly. Being frail, fallible, imperfect human beings, we are quick to anger, quick to blame, slow to forgive, and even slower to forget. No matter. Forgiveness, although difficult, is God's way.

As a teacher, you have been placed in a position of leadership; you serve as an important role model to your students. As such, you must strive to be a model of forgiveness, both inside the classroom and out—no exceptions.

If there exists even one person, alive or dead, whom you have not forgiven (and that includes yourself), follow God's commandment and His will for your life: forgive. Hatred and bitterness and regret are not part of God's plan for your life. Forgiveness is.

If Jesus forgave those who nailed Him to the Cross, and if God forgives you and me, how can you withhold your forgiveness from someone else?

Anne Graham Lotz

— A Prayer —

Lord, just as You have forgiven me, I am going to forgive others. When I forgive others, I not only obey Your commandments, but I also free myself from bitterness and regret. Forgiveness is Your way, Lord, and I will make it my way, too.

Amen

Generosity

It is well with the man who deals generously and lends.

Psalm 112:5 RSV

Each person should do as he has decided in his heart—
not out of regret or out of necessity,
for God loves a cheerful giver.

2 Corinthians 9:7 HCSB

The generous soul will be made rich,
and he who waters will also be watered himself.

Proverbs 11:25 NKJV

Above all, love each other deeply,
because love covers a multitude of sins.

1 Peter 4:8 NIV

I tell you the truth, whatever you did for one of the least of
these brothers of mine, you did for me.

Matthew 25:40 NIV

The words of Jesus are clear: "Freely you have received, freely give" (Matthew 10:8 NIV). As followers of Christ, we are commanded to be generous with our friends, with our families, and with those in need. We must give freely of our time, our possessions, and, most especially, our love.

In 2 Corinthians 9:7, Paul reminds us that when we sow the seeds of generosity, we reap bountiful rewards in accordance with God's plan for our lives. But Paul offers a word of caution: We are commanded to be cheerful givers—not to give "grudgingly or under compulsion."

Today, take God's words to heart and make this pledge: Be a cheerful, generous, courageous giver. The world needs your help, and you need the spiritual rewards that will be yours when you give it.

The mark of a Christian is that he will walk
the second mile and turn the other cheek.
A wise man or woman gives the extra effort,
all for the glory of the Lord Jesus Christ.

John Maxwell

— A Prayer —

Dear Lord, You have been so generous with me; let me be generous with others. Help me to be generous with my time and my possessions as I care for those in need. Help me to teach my students to be cheerful givers, Father, and make us all humble givers, so that the glory and the praise might be Yours.
Amen

Gifts

I remind you to fan into flame the gift of God.

2 Timothy 1:6 NIV

*Every good gift and every perfect gift is from above,
and cometh down from the Father of lights.*

James 1:17 KJV

*Now there are varieties of gifts, but the same Spirit.
And there are varieties of ministries, and the same Lord.*

1 Corinthians 12:4, 5 NASB

*God has given gifts to each of you from his great variety
of spiritual gifts. Manage them well so that God's generosity
can flow through you.*

1 Peter 4:10 NLT

*Since we have gifts that differ according to the grace given to
us, let each exercise them accordingly: if prophecy,
according to the proportion of his faith; if service,
in his serving; or he who teaches, in his teaching;
or he who exhorts, in his exhortation; he who gives,
with liberality; he who leads, with diligence;
he who shows mercy, with cheerfulness.*

Romans 12:6-8 NASB

Perhaps you are one of those lucky teachers who has a natural gift for leading a class. But, even if you have the oratorical abilities of Winston Churchill and the intellectual capacities of Albert Einstein, you can still improve your teaching skills . . . and you should.

God's gifts are no guarantee of success; they must be cultivated and nurtured; otherwise they diminish over time. Today, accept this challenge: value the gift that God has given you, nourish it, make it grow, and share it with your students and with the world. After all, the best way to say "Thank You" for God's gifts is to use them.

One thing taught large in the Holy Scriptures is that while God gives His gifts freely, He will require a strict accounting of them at the end of the road. Each man is personally responsible for his store, be it large or small, and will be required to explain his use of it before the judgment seat of Christ.

A. W. Tozer

— A Prayer —

Heavenly Father, Your gifts to me are priceless
and eternal. I praise You and give thanks for
Your creation, for Your Son, and for the unique talents
and opportunities that You have given me.
Let me use my gifts for the glory of Your Kingdom,
this day and every day.
Amen

God's Blessings

*I pray also that you will have greater understanding in
your heart so you will know the hope to which he has called
us and that you will know how rich and glorious are
the blessings God has promised his holy people. And you will
know that God's power is very great for us who believe.*
Ephesians 1:18, 19 NCV

*For surely, O LORD, you bless the righteous;
you surround them with your favor as with a shield.*
Psalm 5:12 NIV

*I will bless them and the places surrounding my hill.
I will send down showers in season;
there will be showers of blessings.*
Ezekiel 34:26 NIV

Blessings crown the head of the righteous . . . .
Proverbs 10:6 NIV

*I will make you into a great nation and I will bless you;
I will make your name great, and you will be a blessing.
I will bless those who bless you, and whoever curses you
I will curse; and all peoples on earth will be
blessed through you.*
Genesis 12:2, 3 NIV

Have you counted your blessings lately? You should. Of course, God's gifts are too numerous to count, but as a grateful Christian, you should attempt to count them nonetheless.

Your blessings include life, family, friends, career, talents, and possessions, for starters. And your greatest gift—a treasure that was paid for on the cross and is yours for the asking—is God's gift of salvation through Christ Jesus.

Today, give thanks for your blessings and share them. When you do, God will smile . . . and so will your students.

God's kindness is not like the sunset—
brilliant in its intensity, but dying every second.
God's generosity keeps coming and coming and coming.
Bill Hybels

— A Prayer —

Today, Lord, let me count my blessings with
thanksgiving in my heart. You have cared for me,
Lord, and I will give You the glory and the praise.
Let me accept Your blessings and Your gifts,
and let me share them with my students,
just as You first shared them with me.
Amen

God's Commandments

This is how we are sure that we have come to know Him:
by keeping His commands.

1 John 2:3 HCSB

Jesus answered and said unto him, If a man love me,
he will keep my words: and my Father will love him, and
we will come unto him, and make our abode with him.

John 14:23 KJV

Happy are those who fear the Lord. Yes, happy are those
who delight in doing what he commands.

Psalm 112:1 NLT

For this is the love of God, that we keep
his commandments . . . .

1 John 5:3 KJV

Whoso despiseth the word shall be destroyed:
but he that feareth the commandment shall be rewarded.

Proverbs 13:13 KJV

I shall delight in Your commandments, which I love.

Psalm 119:47 NASB

God has given us a guidebook for righteous living called the Holy Bible. It contains thorough instructions which, if followed, lead to fulfillment, righteousness, and salvation. But, if we choose to ignore God's commandments, the results are as predictable as they are tragic. Let us follow God's commandments, and let us conduct our lives in such a way that we might be shining examples to our families, to our friends, to our students, and to the world.

Believe and do what God says.
The life-changing consequences will be limitless, and
the results will be confidence and peace of mind.

Franklin Graham

— A Prayer —

Lord, Your commandments are a perfect guide for
my life; let me obey them, and let me teach others to do
the same. Give me the wisdom to walk righteously
in Your way, Dear Lord, trusting always in You.
Amen

God's Grace

*Grace to you and peace from God our Father
and the Lord Jesus Christ.*

Philippians 1:2 NASB

*For all have sinned and fall short of the glory of God,
and are justified freely by his grace through the redemption
that came by Christ Jesus.*

Romans 3:23, 24 NIV

*You therefore, my son, be strong in the grace
that is in Christ Jesus.*

2 Timothy 2:1 NKJV

*And God raised us up with Christ and seated us with him
in the heavenly realms in Christ Jesus, in order that in
the coming ages he might show the incomparable riches of
his grace, expressed in his kindness to us in Christ Jesus.*

Ephesians 2:6, 7 NIV

*My grace is sufficient for you,
for my power is made perfect in weakness.*

2 Corinthians 12:9 NIV

We have received countless gifts from God, but none can compare with the gift of salvation. When we accept Christ into our hearts, we are saved by God's grace. The familiar words of Ephesians 2:8 make God's promise perfectly clear: we are saved, not by our actions, but by God's mercy. We are saved, not because of our good deeds, but because of our faith in Christ.

God's grace is the ultimate gift, and we owe Him the ultimate in thanksgiving. Let us praise the Creator for His priceless gift, and let us share the Good News with all who cross our paths. We return our Father's love by accepting His grace and by sharing His message and His love. When we do, we are blessed here on earth and throughout all eternity.

Though the details may differ from story to story,
we are all sinners—
saved only by the wonderful grace of God.

Gloria Gaither

— A Prayer —

Dear Lord, You have offered Your grace freely through
Christ Jesus. I praise You for that priceless gift.
Let me share the good news of Your Son with a world
that desperately needs His peace, His abundance,
His love, and His salvation.

Amen

God's Love

We love Him because He first loved us.

1 John 4:19 NKJV

*This is how much God loved the world: He gave his Son,
his one and only Son. And this is why:
so that no one need be destroyed; by believing in him
anyone can have a whole and lasting life.*

John 3:16 MSG

*For he chose us in him before the creation of the world
to be holy and blameless in his sight. In love he predestined us
to be adopted as his sons through Jesus Christ,
in accordance with his pleasure and will . . . .*

Ephesians 1:4, 5 NIV

*But God demonstrates his own love for us in this:
While we were still sinners, Christ died for us.*

Romans 5:8 NIV

His banner over me was love.

Song of Solomon 2:4 KJV

God's love changes lives. And as Christian teachers who have received the priceless gift of God's grace, we must make certain that our students can clearly see the changes that God has made in us. Can we be perfect teachers? Of course not. Can we, at all times, be patient, kind, calm, and loving? That's highly unlikely. What we *can* do is this: we can demonstrate to our students that Christ's love does indeed make a difference in the lives of those who accept Him as their Savior.

God's grace is the ultimate gift, and we owe Him the ultimate in thanksgiving. Let us praise the Creator for His priceless gift; let us share His Good News; and let us live according to His commandments. When we do, our students will be blessed with powerful, godly role models. And we teachers will be transformed, not only for a day, but also for all eternity.

God proved his love on the cross.
When Christ hung, and bled, and died,
it was God saying to the world—I love you.

Billy Graham

— A Prayer —

Dear Lord, for the love You have shown me and the blessings You have given me, I thank You and I praise You. Your Son died so that I might receive the blessing of eternal love and eternal life. I will praise You today, tomorrow, and forever, Lord, for Your love, for Your mercy, and for Your Son.

Amen

God's Mercy

*Therefore let us approach the throne of grace with boldness,
so that we may receive mercy and find grace to help us
at the proper time.*

Hebrews 4:16 HCSB

*Praise be to the God and Father of our Lord Jesus Christ!
In his great mercy he has given us new birth into a living hope
through the resurrection of Jesus Christ from the dead . . . .*

1 Peter 1:3 NIV

The Lord is full of compassion and mercy.

James 5:11 NIV

*But because of his great love for us, God, who is rich in
mercy, made us alive with Christ even when we were dead
in transgressions—it is by grace you have been saved.*

Ephesians 2:4, 5 NIV

*But the mercy of the LORD is from everlasting to everlasting
upon them that fear him, and his righteousness unto
children's children . . . .*

Psalm 103:17 KJV

Romans 3:23 reminds us of a universal truth: "All have sinned, and come short of the glory of God . . . ." (KJV). And, despite our imperfections, God sent His Son to die for our sins. As Christians, we have been blessed by a merciful, loving God, and one way that we thank God is to share His love and His mercy with our students and with all others whom God chooses to place in our paths.

We must appropriate the tender mercy of God
every day after conversion, or problems quickly develop.
We need his grace daily in order to live a righteous life.
Jim Cymbala

— A Prayer —

Thank You, Lord, for Your love. Your love is boundless, infinite, and eternal. Today, let me pause and reflect upon Your love for me, and let me share that love with all those who cross my path. And, as an expression of my love for You, Father, let me share the saving message of Your Son with a world in desperate need of His peace.

Amen

God's Provision

And God will generously provide all you need.
Then you will always have everything you need
and plenty left over to share with others.

2 Corinthians 9:8 NLT

Steep your life in God-reality, God-initiative,
God-provisions. Don't worry about missing out.
You'll find all your everyday human concerns will be met.

Matthew 6:33 MSG

I will lift up my eyes to the mountains; from whence shall
my help come? My help comes from the Lord,
who made the heaven and earth.

Psalm 121:1, 2 NASB

But my God shall supply all your need according to his riches
in glory by Christ Jesus.

Philippians 4:19 KJV

So, what do you think? With God on our side like this,
how can we lose? If God didn't hesitate to put everything on
the line for us, embracing our condition and exposing himself
to the worst by sending his own Son, is there anything else
he wouldn't gladly and freely do for us?

Romans 8:31, 32 MSG

In a world filled with dangers and temptations, God is the ultimate armor. In a world filled with misleading messages, God's Word is the ultimate truth. In a world filled with more frustrations than we can count, God's Son offers the ultimate peace. Will you accept God's peace and wear God's armor against the dangers of our world?

Sometimes, in the crush of everyday life, God may seem far away, but He is not. He is with you night and day; He knows your thoughts and your prayers. God is your ultimate Protector. And, when you earnestly seek His protection, you will find it because He is here—always—waiting patiently for you to reach out to Him.

We have ample evidence that the Lord is able to guide.
The promises cover every imaginable situation.
All we need to do is to take the hand he stretches out.

Elisabeth Elliot

— A Prayer —

Lord, You have promised that You will provide for my needs, and I trust that promise. But sometimes, because of my imperfect faith, I fall prey to worry and doubt. Today, give me the courage to trust You completely. You are my protector, dear Lord; let me praise You, let me love You, and let me trust in the perfect wisdom of Your plan.

Amen

God's Timing

I trust in You, O LORD, I say, "You are my God."
My times are in Your hand.

Psalm 31:14, 15 NASB

This is what the LORD says: "In the time of my favor I will
answer you, and in the day of salvation I will help you . . . .

Isaiah 49:8 NIV

He has made everything beautiful in its time.
He has also set eternity in the hearts of men;
yet they cannot fathom what God has done
from beginning to end.

Ecclesiastes 3:11 NIV

Yet the LORD longs to be gracious to you;
he rises to show you compassion.
For the LORD is a God of justice.
Blessed are all who wait for him!

Isaiah 30:18 NIV

I waited patiently for the Lord;
And He inclined to me, And heard my cry.

Psalm 40:1 NKJV

Students, as a whole, can be quite impatient. They can't wait for class to end; ditto for the school day and the school week. They wait impatiently for Christmas vacation, spring break, and—most urgently—summer vacation. But, wise teachers understand that life beyond the classroom requires patience, patience, and more patience.

Unlike the precisely charted school year, life unfolds according to a timetable that is ordained, not by man, but by God. Let us, as believers, wait patiently for God, and let us teach patience to those who look to us for guidance . . . even if they're squirming in their seats, waiting for the bell to ring.

God is in no hurry. Compared to the works of mankind,
He is extremely deliberate.
God is not a slave to the human clock.

Charles Swindoll

— A Prayer —

Dear Lord, Your wisdom is infinite, and the timing of
Your Heavenly plan is perfect. You have a plan for
my life that is grander than I can imagine. When I am
impatient, remind me that You are never early or late.
You are always on time, Father, so let me trust in You.

Amen

God's Will

The world and its desires pass away,
but the man who does the will of God lives forever.

1 John 2:17 NIV

Who are those who fear the Lord? He will show them
the path they should choose. They will live in prosperity, and
their children will inherit the Promised Land.

Psalm 25:12, 13 NLT

"Father, if it is Your will, take this cup away from Me;
nevertheless not My will, but Yours, be done."

Luke 22:42 NKJV

The steps of the Godly are directed by the Lord.
He delights in every detail of their lives.
Though they stumble, they will not fall,
for the Lord holds them by the hand.

Psalm 37:23, 24 NLT

It is God who works in you to will and
to act according to his good purpose.

Philippians 2:13 NIV

God has important plans for your life *and* for the lives of your students. But He won't force His plans upon you. To the contrary, He has given all of His children free will (a fact that is not lost on any teacher who has ever tried to quiet an unruly classroom).

While you, as a concerned teacher, can encourage your students to seek purpose and meaning for their own lives, you can't force them to do so. You can, however, seek to discover God's plan for *your* life. God is listening and waiting for you to reach out to Him, and He intends to use you in wonderful, unexpected ways. So let Him.

If you want to know the will and voice of God, you must give the time and effort to cultivate a love relationship with Him. That is what He wants!

Henry Blackaby

— A Prayer —

Heavenly Father, in these quiet moments before this busy day unfolds, I come to You. I will study Your Word and seek Your guidance. Give me the wisdom to know Your will for my life and the courage to follow wherever You may lead me, today and forever.

Amen

God's Word

But He answered, "It is written:
Man must not live on bread alone,
but on every word that comes from the mouth of God."

Matthew 4:4 HCSB

Blessed are those who hunger and thirst for righteousness,
for they will be filled.

Matthew 5:6 NIV

For the word of God is living and active.
Sharper than any double-edged sword, it penetrates even to
dividing soul and spirit, joints and marrow;
it judges the thoughts and attitudes of the heart.

Hebrews 4:12 NIV

Your word is a lamp to my feet and a light for my path.

Psalm 119:105 NIV

Heaven and earth will pass away,
but my words will never pass away.

Matthew 24:35 NIV

Is God's Word a lamp that guides your path? Is God's Word your indispensable compass for everyday living, or is it relegated to Sunday morning services? Do you read the Bible faithfully or sporadically? The answer to these questions will determine the direction of your thoughts, the direction of your day, and the direction of your life.

God's Word can be a roadmap to a place of righteousness and abundance. Make it *your* roadmap. God's wisdom can be a light to guide your steps. Claim it as *your* light today, tomorrow, and every day of your life—and then walk confidently in the footsteps of God's only begotten Son.

If we are not continually fed with God's Word,
we will starve spiritually.

Stormie Omartian

— A Prayer —

Heavenly Father, Your Holy Word is a light unto
the world; let me study it, trust it, and share.
In all that I do, help me be a worthy witness for
You as I share the Good News of
Your perfect Son and Your perfect Word.
Amen

Golden Rule

See that no one renders evil for evil to anyone,
but always pursue what is good both
for yourselves and for all.

1 Thessalonians 5:15 NKJV

Let us not become weary in doing good, for at the proper
time we will reap a harvest if we do not give up.

Galatians 6:9 NIV

Each of you should look not only to your own interests,
but also to the interest of others.

Philippians 2:4 NIV

Here is a simple, rule-of-thumb for behavior:
Ask yourself what you want people to do for you,
then grab the initiative and do it for them.
Add up God's Law and Prophets and this is what you get.

Matthew 7:12 MSG

Give to everyone who asks you,
and if anyone takes what belongs to you,
do not demand it back.

Luke 6:30 NIV

The words of Matthew 7:12 remind us that, as believers in Christ, we are commanded to treat others as we wish to be treated. This commandment is, indeed, the Golden Rule for Christians of every generation. When we weave the thread of kindness into the very fabric of our lives, we give glory to the One who gave His life for ours.

Because we are imperfect human beings, we are, on occasion, selfish, thoughtless, or cruel. But God commands us to behave otherwise. He teaches us to rise above our own imperfections and to treat others with unselfishness and love. When we observe God's Golden Rule, we help build His kingdom here on earth. And, when we share the love of Christ, we share a priceless gift; may we share it today and every day that we live.

> The Golden Rule starts at home,
> but it should never stop there.
>
> *Marie T. Freeman*

— A Prayer —

Dear Lord, let me teach the Golden Rule, and let me live by it. Because I expect kindness, let me be kind. Because I wish to be loved, let me be loving. Because I need forgiveness, let me be merciful. In all things, Lord, let me live by the Golden Rule that is the commandment of Your Son Jesus.

Amen

Gratitude

Be cheerful no matter what; pray all the time;
thank God no matter what happens.
This is the way God wants you who belong
to Christ Jesus to live.

1 Thessalonians 5:16-18 MSG

Enter his gates with thanksgiving, go into his courts
with praise. Give thanks to him and bless his name.

Psalm 100:4 NLT

Everything created by God is good, and nothing is to be
rejected, if it is received with gratitude; for it is sanctified by
means of the word of God and prayer.

1 Timothy 4:4, 5 NASB

Therefore, since we receive a kingdom which cannot be
shaken, let us show gratitude, by which we may offer
to God an acceptable service with reverence and awe . . . .

Hebrews 12:28 NASB

As teachers, we have responsibilities that begin long before the school bell rings and end long after the last student has left the classroom. Amid the hustle and bustle of the daily grind, it is easy to lose sight of God and His blessings. But, when we forget to slow down and say "Thank You" to our Creator, we rob ourselves of His presence, His peace, and His joy.

Our task, as believing Christians, is to praise God many times each day. Then, with gratitude in our hearts, we can face our daily duties with the perspective and power that only He can provide.

It is only with gratitude that life becomes rich.

Dietrich Bonhoeffer

— A Prayer —

Lord, let my attitude be one of gratitude.
You have given me much; when I think of Your grace
and goodness, I am humbled and thankful.
Today, let me express my thanksgiving, Father,
not just through my words but also through my deeds . . .
and may all the glory be Yours.

Amen

Happiness

Those who are pure in their thinking are happy,
because they will be with God.

Matthew 5:8 NCV

A cheerful heart is good medicine . . . .

Proverbs 17:22 NIV

How happy are those who can live in your house,
always singing your praises.
How happy are those who are strong in the Lord . . . .

Psalm 84:4, 5 NLT

The cheerful heart has a continual feast.

Proverbs 15:15 NIV

God loves a cheerful giver.

2 Corinthians 9:7 NIV

Happiness depends less upon our circumstances than upon our thoughts. When we turn our thoughts to God, to His gifts, and to His glorious creation, we experience the joy that God intends for His children. But, when we focus on the negative aspects of life, we suffer needlessly.

Do you sincerely want to be a happy Christian? Then set your mind and your heart upon God's love and His grace. The fullness of life in Christ is available to all who seek it and claim it. Count yourself among that number. Seek first the salvation that is available through a personal relationship with Jesus Christ, and then claim the joy, the peace, and the spiritual abundance that the Shepherd offers His sheep.

The happiest people in the world are not those
who have no problems, but the people who have learned
to live with those things that are less than perfect.

James Dobson

Lord, let me be a teacher who celebrates life.
Let me rejoice in the gift of this day, and let me
praise You for the gift of Your Son. Let me be a joyful
Christian, Lord, as I share Your Good News with friends,
with family, and with the world.
Amen

Holiness

But now you must be holy in everything you do,
just as God—who chose you to be his children—is holy.
For he himself has said,
"You must be holy because I am holy."

1 Peter 1:15, 16 NLT

Therefore come out from them and be separate,
says the Lord. Touch no unclean thing,
and I will receive you.

2 Corinthians 6:17 NIV

Blessed are the pure of heart, for they will see God.

Matthew 5:8 NIV

The Lord will not reject his people; he will not abandon
his own special possession. Judgement will come again for
the righteous, and those who are upright will have a reward.

Psalm 94:14, 15 NLT

The righteous shall flourish like the palm tree:
he shall grow like a cedar in Lebanon.

Psalm 92:12 KJV

As Christians, we are called to walk with God and to obey His commandments. But, we live in a world that presents countless temptations for adults and *even more* temptations for our students.

As leaders in the classroom, we must teach our students that the choices they make are never without consequence. When they choose wisely, they reap bountiful rewards. But, when they behave foolishly, they invite pain and disappointment into their lives.

As Christian teachers, we must instruct our students by word and by example. And our instructions from God are clear: When confronted with sin, we must walk—or better yet run—in the opposite direction. When we do, we reap the blessings that God has promised to all those who live according to His will and His Word.

A life growing in its purity and devotion
will be a more prayerful life.

E. M. Bounds

— A Prayer —

Dear Lord, this world is filled with so many temptations, distractions, and frustrations. When I turn my thoughts away from You and Your Word, I suffer. But when I turn my thoughts, my faith, and my prayers to You, I am safe.
Direct my path, Father, and let me discover
Your will for me today and every day that I live.

Amen

Honesty

In every way be an example of doing good deeds.
When you teach, do it with honesty and seriousness.

Titus 2:7 NCV

Therefore, since we have this ministry, as we have received
mercy, we do not lose heart. But we have renounced
the hidden things of shame, not walking in craftiness nor
handling the word of God deceitfully, but by manifestation of
the truth commending ourselves to every
man's conscience in the sight of God.

2 Corinthians 4:1, 2 NKJV

The Lord detests lying lips,
but he delights in men who are truthful.

Proverbs 12:22 NIV

But when he, the Spirit of truth, comes,
he will guide you into all truth . . . .

John 16:13 NIV

Jesus answered, "I am the way and the truth and the life.
No one comes to the Father except through me."

John 14:6 NIV

From the time we are children, we are taught that honesty is the best policy. And, in the classroom, we instruct our students that honesty is also the school's policy. But, honesty is not just *the best* policy or *the school's* policy, it is also *God's* policy. If we are to be servants worthy of His holy blessings, we must remember that truth is not just the best way, it is God's way. May we teach truth and practice it . . . but not necessarily in that order.

God doesn't expect you to be perfect,
but he does insist on complete honesty.

Rick Warren

— A Prayer —

Dear Lord, let me walk in truth and let me share Your truth. As a teacher, I am a role model to my students. Make me Your worthy servant so that others might see my love for You reflected in my words and my deeds.

Amen

Hope

Let us hold on to the confession of our hope without wavering, for He who promised is faithful.

Hebrews 10:23 HCSB

Be of good courage, and he shall strengthen your heart, all ye that hope in the LORD.

Psalm 31:24 KJV

Know that wisdom is sweet to your soul; if you find it, there is a future hope for you, and your hope will not be cut off.

Proverbs 24:14 NIV

The Lord is good to those whose hope is in him, to the one who seeks him; it is good to wait quietly for the salvation of the Lord.

Lamentations 3:25, 26 NIV

May the God of hope fill you with all joy and peace as you trust in him, so that you may overflow with hope by the power of the Holy Spirit.

Romans 15:13 NIV

The hope that the world offers is fleeting and imperfect. The hope that God offers is unchanging, unshakable, and unending. It is no wonder, then, that when we seek security from worldly sources, our hopes are often dashed. Thankfully, God has no such record of failure.

Where will you place your hopes today? Will you entrust your future to man or to God? Will you seek solace exclusively from fallible human beings, or will you place your hopes, first and foremost, in the trusting hands of your Creator? The decision is yours, and you must live with the results of the choice you make.

For thoughtful believers, hope begins with God. So today, as you embark upon the next stage of your life's journey, consider the words of the Psalmist: "You are my hope; O Lord GOD, You are my confidence" (71:5 NASB). Then, place your trust in the One who cannot be shaken.

Easter comes each year to remind us of a truth that is eternal and universal. The empty tomb of Easter morning says to you and me, "Of course you'll encounter trouble. But behold a God of power who can take any evil and turn it into a door of hope."

Catherine Marshall

— A Prayer —

Dear Lord, make me a teacher of hope. If I become discouraged, let me turn to You. If I grow weary, let me seek strength in You. When I face adversity, let me seek Your will and trust Your Word. In every aspect of my life, I will trust You, Father, so that my heart will be filled with faith and hope, this day and forever.

Amen

Integrity

The godly walk with integrity;
blessed are their children after them.

Proverbs 20:7 NLT

Till I die, I will not deny my integrity.
I will maintain my righteousness and never let go of it;
my conscience will not reproach me as long as I live.

Job 27:5, 6 NIV

The man of integrity walks securely,
but he who takes crooked paths will be found out.

Proverbs 10:9 NIV

In all things showing yourself to be a pattern of good works;
in doctrine showing integrity,
reverence, incorruptibility . . . .

Titus 2:7 NKJV

As in water face reflects face,
so the heart of man reflects man.

Proverbs 27:19 NASB

Wise teachers understand the importance of character . . . and teach it. Character is built slowly over a lifetime. It is the sum of every right decision, every honest word, every noble thought, and every heartfelt prayer. It is forged on the anvil of honorable work and polished by the twin virtues of generosity and humility. Character is a precious thing—difficult to build but easy to tear down; godly teachers value it and protect it at all costs . . . and they encourage their students to do the same.

God never called us to naïveté.
He called us to integrity . . . . The biblical concept of integrity emphasizes mature innocence not childlike ignorance.

Beth Moore

— A Prayer —

Heavenly Father, Your Word instructs me to walk
in integrity and in truth. Make me a worthy teacher,
Lord. Let my words be true, and let my actions
lead my students to You.
Amen

Jesus

For Jesus is the one referred to in the Scriptures,
where it says, "The stone that you builders rejected has now
become the cornerstone." There is salvation in no one else!
There is no other name in all of heaven
for people to call on to save them.

Acts 4:11, 12 NLT

Jesus Christ is the same yesterday, today, and forever.

Hebrews 13:8 HCSB

Jesus answered them, "I told you, and you do not believe;
the works that I do in My Father's name,
these testify of Me . . . I and the Father are one."

John 10:25, 30 NASB

I am the Vine, you are the branches. When you're joined
with me and I with you, the relation intimate and organic,
the harvest is sure to be abundant.

John 15:5 MSG

For the Son of man is come to save that which was lost.

Matthew 18:11 KJV

Our circumstances change but Jesus does not. Even when the world seems to be trembling beneath our feet, Jesus remains the spiritual bedrock that cannot be moved.

The old familiar hymn begins, "What a friend we have in Jesus . . . ." No truer words were ever penned. Jesus is the sovereign friend and ultimate savior of mankind. Christ showed enduring love for His believers by willingly sacrificing His own life so that we might have eternal life. Let us love Him, praise Him, and share His message of salvation with our neighbors and with the world.

Had Jesus been the Word become word,
He would have spun theories about life, but since
he was the Word become flesh, he put shoes on
all his theories and made them walk.

E. Stanley Jones

— A Prayer —

Dear Heavenly Father, I praise You and thank You
for Your priceless gift: Jesus Christ. Let me share
the Good News of the One who became a man so that
I might become His, not only for today, but also for
all eternity. Jesus is my savior and my strength.
I will welcome Him into my heart with love and
thanksgiving, today and forever.

Amen

Jesus' Love

Just as the Father has loved Me, I have also loved you;
abide in My love.

John 15:9 NASB

Greater love has no one than this,
that he lay down his life for his friends.

John 15:13 NIV

Do you think anyone is going to be able to drive a wedge
between us and Christ's love for us? There is no way!
Not trouble, not hard times, not hatred, not hunger,
not homelessness, not bullying threats, not backstabbing,
not even the worst sins listed in Scripture . . . I'm absolutely
convinced that nothing, nothing living or dead, angelic or
demonic, today or tomorrow, high or low, thinkable or
unthinkable, absolutely nothing can get between us
and God's love because of the way that
Jesus our Master has embraced us.

Romans 8:35, 38, 39 MSG

I am the good shepherd.
The good shepherd lays down his life for the sheep.

John 10:11 NIV

How much does Christ love us? More than we, as mere mortals, can comprehend. His love is perfect and steadfast. Even though we are fallible and wayward, the Good Shepherd cares for us still. Even though we have fallen far short of the Father's commandments, Christ loves us with a power and depth that is beyond our understanding. The sacrifice that Jesus made upon the cross was made for each of us, and His love endures to the edge of eternity and beyond.

Christ's love changes everything. When we accept His gift of grace, we are transformed, not only for today, but forever. Yes, Christ's love changes everything. May we invite Him into our hearts so it can then change everything *in us*.

Jesus loves me! This I know, for the Bible tells me so.
Little ones to him belong; they are weak, but he is
strong. Yes, Jesus loves me! Yes, Jesus loves me!
Yes, Jesus loves me! The Bible tells me so.
Anna B. Warner and Susan Warner

— A Prayer —

Dear Jesus, You are my Savior and my protector.
Give me the courage to trust You completely. Today,
I will praise You, I will honor You, and I will live
according to Your commandments, so that thorough me,
others might come to know Your perfect love.

Amen

Joy

These things I have spoken to you,
that My joy may remain in you,
and that your joy may be full.

John 15:11 NKJV

So you also have sorrow now. But I will see you again.
Your hearts will rejoice, and no one will rob you of your joy.

John 16:22 HCSB

Always be full of joy in the Lord. I say it again—rejoice!

Philippians 4:4 NLT

Shout for joy to the LORD, all the earth.
Worship the LORD with gladness;
come before him with joyful songs.

Psalm 100:1, 2 NIV

This is the day the LORD has made;
let us rejoice and be glad in it.

Psalm 118:24 NIV

Christ made it clear to His followers: He intended that His joy would become their joy. And it still holds true today: Christ intends that His believers share His love with His joy in their hearts. Today, whether you find yourself inside the classroom or outside it, share the joy that you feel in *your* heart, just as Christ freely shared His joy with you.

God knows everything. He can manage everything,
and He loves us. Surely this is enough
for a fullness of joy that is beyond words.
Hannah Whitall Smith

— A Prayer —

Lord, make me a joyous Christian.
Because of my salvation through Your Son,
I have every reason to celebrate—let my joy be
evident in every aspect of life, including my life inside
the classroom. Today, let my words and deeds
be a testimony to Christ's love and to His grace.
Amen

The Joy of Teaching

You will teach me how to live a holy life.
Being with you will fill me with joy;
at your right hand I will find pleasure forever.

Psalm 16:11 NCV

We all have different gifts, each of which came because of
the grace God gave us. The person who has the gift of
prophecy should use that gift in agreement with the faith.
Anyone who has the gift of serving should serve. Anyone
who has the gift of teaching should teach. Whoever has
the gift of encouraging others should encourage.
Whoever has the gift of giving to others should give freely.
Anyone who has the gift of being a leader should try hard
when he leads. Whoever has the gift of showing mercy to
others should do so with joy.

Romans 12:6-8 NCV

Light shines on the godly, and joy on those who do right.
May all who are godly be happy in the Lord
and praise his holy name.

Psalm 97:11, 12 NLT

Teaching should be a joyful experience, but every teacher knows that some days are so busy and so hurried that abundance seems a distant promise. It is not. Every day, we can claim the spiritual abundance and joy that God promises for our lives . . . and we should.

C. H. Spurgeon, the renowned 19th century English clergymen, advised, "Rejoicing is clearly a spiritual command. To ignore it, I need to remind you, is disobedience." As Christians, we are called by our Creator to live abundantly, prayerfully, and joyfully. To do otherwise is to squander His spiritual gifts.

If, today, your heart is heavy, open the door of your soul to the Father and to His only begotten Son. Christ offers you His peace and His joy. Accept it and share it freely, just as Christ has freely shared His joy with you.

Our sense of joy, satisfaction, and fulfillment in life
increases, no matter what the circumstances,
if we are in the center of God's will.

Billy Graham

— A Prayer —

Dear Lord, You have given me so many blessings; let me celebrate Your gifts. I praise You, Father, for the gift of Your Son and for the priceless gift of salvation. Make me be a joyful Christian, a worthy example to my students, and a dutiful servant to You, this day and forever.

Amen

Kindness

And be kind and compassionate to one another,
forgiving one another,
just as God also forgave you in Christ.

Ephesians 4:32 HCSB

Refuse to get involved in inane discussions;
they always end up in fights. God's servant must not
be argumentative, but a gentle listener and a teacher
who keeps cool, working firmly but patiently with
those who refuse to obey.

2 Timothy 2:23, 24 MSG

A gentle answer turns away wrath,
but a harsh word stirs up anger.

Proverbs 15:1 NIV

A kind person is doing himself a favor.
But a cruel person brings trouble upon himself.

Proverbs 11:17 ICB

In the busyness and stress of a teacher's demanding day, it is easy to become frustrated. We are imperfect human beings struggling to manage our lives as best we can, but sometimes we fall short. When we are distracted or disappointed, we may neglect to share a kind word or a kind deed. This oversight hurts others, and it hurts us as well.

Christ's words are straightforward: "I tell you the truth, anything you did for even the least of my people here, you also did for me" (Matthew 25:40 NCV). For believers, then, the message is clear: When we share a word of encouragement with a student or extend the hand of friendship to a peer, God smiles.

Do all the good you can. By all the means you can.
In all the ways you can. In all the places you can.
At all the times you can. To all the people you can.
As long as ever you can.

John Wesley

— A Prayer —

Lord, make me a loving, encouraging Christian.
And, let my love for Christ be reflected through
the kindness that I show to my students, to my family,
to my friends, and to all who need
the healing touch of the Master's hand.

Amen

Laughter

A cheerful heart is good medicine.

Proverbs 17:22 NIV

There is a time for everything, and a season for every activity under heaven . . . a time to weep and a time to laugh, a time to mourn and a time to dance . . . .

Ecclesiastes 3:1, 4 NIV

Shout for joy to the LORD, all the earth, burst into jubilant song with music; make music to the LORD with the harp, with the harp and the sound of singing, with trumpets and the blast of the ram's horn— shout for joy before the LORD, the King.

Psalm 98:4-6 NIV

Nehemiah said, "Go and enjoy choice food and sweet drinks, and send some to those who have nothing prepared. This day is sacred to our Lord. Do not grieve, for the joy of the LORD is your strength."

Nehemiah 8:10 NIV

L aughter is medicine for the soul, but sometimes, amid the stresses of the day, we forget to take our medicine. Instead of viewing our world with a mixture of optimism and humor, we allow worries and distractions to rob us of the joy that God intends for our lives.

Today, as you go about your daily activities, approach life with a smile on your lips and hope in your heart. And laugh every chance you get. After all, God created laughter for a reason . . . and Father indeed knows best. So laugh!

I think everybody ought to be a laughing Christian.
I'm convinced that there's just one place
where there's not any laughter, and that's hell.

Jerry Clower

— A Prayer —

Dear Lord, laughter is Your gift. Today and every day,
put a smile on my face, and let me share that smile
with all my students . . . and let me laugh.
Amen

Leadership

Shepherd God's flock, for whom you are responsible.
Watch over them because you want to,
not because you are forced. That is how God wants it.
Do it because you are happy to serve.

1 Peter 5:2 NCV

We have different gifts, according to the grace given us.
If a man's gift is prophesying, let him use it in proportion to
his faith. If it is serving, let him serve; if it is teaching,
let him teach; if it is encouraging, let him encourage;
if it is contributing to the needs of others,
let him give generously; if it is leadership,
let him govern diligently; if it is showing mercy,
let him do it cheerfully.

Romans 12:6-8 NIV

Those who are wise will shine like the brightness of
the heavens, and those who lead many to righteousness,
like the stars for ever and ever.

Daniel 12:3 NIV

As a teacher, you are automatically placed in a position of leadership. Unless you assume firm control over your students, effective learning will not take place in your classroom.

John Maxwell writes, "Great leaders understand that the right attitude will set the right atmosphere, which enables the right response from others." As the leader of your class, it's up to you to set the proper balance between discipline and amusement, between entertainment and scholarship.

Savvy teachers learn to strike an appropriate balance between discipline (which is necessary for maintaining order) and fun (which is necessary for maintaining interest). The rest, of course, is up to the students.

You can never separate a leader's actions
from his character.

John Maxwell

— A Prayer —

Dear Lord, let me be a leader in my classroom
and a worthy example to my students.
Give me wisdom, courage, compassion, and faith.
Let me turn to You, Father, for guidance and
for strength in all that I say and do.
Amen

Learning

A wise man will hear and increase in learning,
and a man of understanding will acquire wise counsel.

Proverbs 1:5 NASB

Whoever gives heed to instruction prospers,
and blessed is he that trusts in the Lord.

Proverbs 16:20 NIV

It is not good to have zeal without knowledge,
nor to be hasty and miss the way.

Proverbs 19:2 NIV

The fear of the Lord is the beginning of knowledge,
but fools despise wisdom and discipline.

Proverbs 1:7 NIV

The lips of the wise spread knowledge;
not so the hearts of fools.

Proverbs 15:7 NIV

Our children need both knowledge and wisdom. Knowledge is found in textbooks. Wisdom, on the other hand, is found in God's Holy Word *and* in the carefully chosen words of loving parents and thoughtful teachers. When we give our children the gift of knowledge, we do them a wonderful service. But, when we share the gift of wisdom, we offer a timeless treasure that surpasses knowledge and reshapes eternity.

The wonderful thing about God's schoolroom is
that we get to grade our own papers. You see,
He doesn't test us so He can learn how well we're doing.
He tests us so *we* can discover how well we're doing.

Charles Swindoll

— A Prayer —

Dear Lord, although I am a teacher,
I still have *so* much to learn. Help me to watch,
to listen, to think, and to learn, every day of my life.
Amen

Life

*Make it your ambition to lead a quiet life, to mind
your own business and to work with your hands, just as
we told you, so that your daily life may win the respect of
outsiders and so that you will not be dependent on anybody.*
1 Thessalonians 4:11, 12 NIV

*Watch your life and doctrine closely.
Persevere in them, because if you do,
you will save both yourself and your hearers.*
1 Timothy 4:16 NIV

*You have made known to me the path of life;
you will fill me with joy in your presence,
with eternal pleasures at your right hand.*
Psalm 16:11 NIV

*His divine power has given us everything we need for life
and godliness through our knowledge of him
who called us by his own glory and goodness.*
2 Peter 1:3 NIV

*I urge you to live a life worthy of the calling
you have received.*
Ephesians 4:1 NIV

Life is God's gift to you, and He intends that you celebrate His glorious gift. If you're a teacher who treasures each day—and if you encourage your students to do the same—you will be blessed by your Father in heaven.

Christian believers face the inevitable challenges and disappointments of each day armed with the joy of Christ and the promise of salvation. So whatever this day holds for you, begin it and end it with God as your partner and Christ as your Savior. And throughout the day, give thanks to the One who created you and saved you. God's love for you is infinite. Accept it joyously and be thankful.

The measure of a life, after all,
is not its duration but its donation.

Corrie ten Boom

— A Prayer —

Lord, You have given me the gift of life.
Let me treasure it, and let me use it for
Your service and for Your glory.
Amen

Loving God

Jesus answered, "If anyone loves Me, he will keep My word.
My Father will love him, and We will come to him
and make Our home with him.

John 14:23 HCSB

Whoever believes that Jesus is the Christ is born of God,
and whoever loves the Father loves the child born of Him.

1 John 5:1 NASB

This is love: not that we loved God, but that he loved us
and sent his Son as an atoning sacrifice for our sins.

1 John 4:10 NIV

Love the LORD your God with all your heart and
with all your soul and with all your strength.

Deuteronomy 6:5 NIV

It is good to praise the LORD and make music to your name,
O Most High, to proclaim your love in the morning
and your faithfulness at night . . . .

Psalm 92:1, 2 NIV

When we worship God with faith and assurance, when we place Him at the absolute center of our lives, we invite His love into our hearts. In turn, we grow to love Him more deeply as we sense His love for us. St. Augustine wrote, "I love you, Lord, not doubtingly, but with absolute certainty. Your Word beat upon my heart until I fell in love with you, and now the universe and everything in it tells me to love you."

Let us pray that we, too, will turn our hearts to our Father, knowing with certainty that He loves us and that we love Him.

The surest evidence of our love to Christ is
obedience to the laws of Christ.
Love is the root, obedience is the fruit.

Matthew Henry

— A Prayer —

Dear Heavenly Father, You have blessed me with
a love that is infinite and eternal. Let me love You, Lord,
more and more each day. Make me a loving servant,
Father, today and throughout eternity.
And, let me show my love for You by sharing
Your message and Your love with others.
Amen

Loving Others

Love each other like brothers and sisters.
Give each other more honor than you want for yourselves.
Romans 12:10 NCV

You have heard that it was said, "Love your neighbor
and hate your enemy." But I tell you:
Love your enemies and pray for those who persecute you.
Matthew 5:43, 44 NIV

And he has given us this command:
Whoever loves God must also love his brother.
1 John 4:21 NIV

Jesus replied, "'Love the Lord your God with all your heart
and with all your soul and with all your mind.'
This is the first and greatest commandment.
And the second is like it: 'Love your neighbor as yourself.'
All the Law and the Prophets hang on
these two commandments."
Matthew 22:37-40 NIV

And the Lord make you to increase and abound in love one
toward another, and toward all men . . . .
1 Thessalonians 3:12 KJV

If we are to follow the commands of our Father in heaven, we must sow seeds of kindness and love. God is love, and kindness is God's commandment. As believers, we are obliged to love *all* our neighbors, not just the loveable ones. So, today, let's be a little kinder than necessary, and let's teach the art of kindness through our words and our deeds. Our students are watching . . . and so, for that matter, is God.

So Jesus came, stripping himself of everything as he came—omnipotence, omniscience, omnipresence—everything except love. "He emptied himself" (Philippians 2:7), emptied himself of everything except love. Love—his only protection, his only weapon, his only method.

E. Stanley Jones

— A Prayer —

Dear Lord, Your love for me is infinite and eternal. Let me acknowledge Your love, accept Your love, and share Your love. Make me a teacher who demonstrates compassion, understanding, and forgiveness. And let the love that I feel in my heart be expressed through kind words, good deeds, and heartfelt prayers.

Amen

Maturity

*When I was a child, I spoke and thought and reasoned
as a child does. But when I grew up,
I put away childish things.*

1 Corinthians 13:11 NLT

*Therefore let us leave the elementary teachings
about Christ and go on to maturity . . . .*

Hebrews 6:1 NIV

*But grow in grace, and in the knowledge of our Lord
and Saviour Jesus Christ . . . .*

2 Peter 3:18 KJV

*Continue in what you have learned and have become
convinced of, because you know those from
whom you learned it, and how from infancy you have known
the holy Scriptures, which are able to make you wise for
salvation through faith in Christ Jesus.*

2 Timothy 3:14, 15 NIV

*I press on toward the goal to win the prize for which
God has called me heavenward in Christ Jesus.*

Philippians 3:14 NIV

If only our students would behave maturely and responsibly, teaching would be a breeze. But, here in the real world, young people don't grow into mature adults overnight. What's a teacher to do? Be patient, be understanding, and be demanding. Teachers who allow undisciplined behavior to go unchecked are doing a disservice to their students. God does not reward laziness nor does He praise mediocrity, and neither should we.

Being a Christian means accepting the terms of creation, accepting God as our maker and redeemer, and growing day by day into an increasingly glorious creature in Christ, developing joy, experiencing love, maturing in peace.

Eugene Peterson

— A Prayer —

Dear Lord, let me grow in Your wisdom. When I study Your Word and follow Your commandments, I become a more mature Christian and a more effective teacher. Let me grow up, Lord, and let me keep growing up every day that I live.

Amen

Miracles

Jesus looked at them and said, "With man this is impossible,
but with God all things are possible."

Matthew 19:26 NIV

But as it is written: "Eye has not seen, nor ear heard,
nor have entered into the heart of man the things which God
has prepared for those who love Him."

1 Corinthians 2:9 NKJV

God also testified to it [salvation] by signs,
wonders and various miracles, and gifts of the Holy Spirit
distributed according to his will.

Hebrews 2:4 NIV

Jesus said to them,
"I have shown you many great miracles from the Father."

John 10:32 NIV

You are the God who performs miracles;
you display your power among the peoples.

Psalm 77:14 NIV

Do you believe in an all-powerful God who can do miraculous things in you and through you? You should. But perhaps, as you have faced the inevitable struggles of life here on earth, you have—without realizing it—placed limitations on God. To do so is a profound mistake. God's power has no such limitations, and He can work mighty miracles in your own life if you let Him.

Do you lack a firm faith in God's power to perform miracles for you and your loved ones? If so, you are attempting to place limitations on a God who has none. Instead of doubting your Heavenly Father, you must place yourself in His hands. Instead of doubting God's power, you must trust it. Expect Him to work miracles, and be watchful. With God, absolutely nothing is impossible, including an amazing assortment of miracles that He stands ready, willing, and perfectly able to perform for you and yours.

Miracles are not contrary to nature,
but only contrary to what we know about nature.
St. Augustine

— A Prayer —

Dear God, nothing is impossible for You. Your infinite power is beyond human understanding—keep me always mindful of Your strength. When I lose hope, give me faith; when others lose hope, let me teach of Your glory and Your works. Today, Lord, let me expect the miraculous, and let me trust in You.

Amen

Missions

*You are a chosen people. You are a kingdom of priests,
God's holy nation, his very own possession. This is so you
can show others the goodness of God, for he called you out of
the darkness into his wonderful light.*

1 Peter 2:9 NLT

*And when the Holy Spirit comes on you, you will be able to
be my witnesses in Jerusalem, all over Judea and Samaria,
even to the ends of the world.
Now then we are ambassadors for Christ . . . .*

Acts 1:8 MSG

*As you go, preach this message:
"The kingdom of heaven is near."*

Matthew 10:7 NIV

*Then Jesus came to them and said, "All authority in
heaven and on earth has been given to me.
Therefore go and make disciples of all nations,
baptizing them in the name of the Father and of the Son
and of the Holy Spirit, and teaching them to obey everything
I have commanded you. And surely I am with you always,
to the very end of the age."*

Matthew 28:18-20 NIV

The Good News of Jesus Christ should be shouted from the rooftops by believers the world over. But all too often, it is not. For a variety of reasons, many Christians keep their beliefs to themselves, and when they do, the world suffers because of their failure to speak up.

As believers, we are called to share the transforming message of Jesus with our families, with our neighbors, and with the world. Jesus commands us to become fishers of men. And, the time to go fishing is now. We must share the Good News of Jesus Christ today—tomorrow may indeed be too late.

Missions is God finding those whose hearts
are right with Him and placing them where they can
make a difference for His kingdom.

Henry Blackaby

— A Prayer —

Lord, make me a missionary for You in word and deed.
Let me teach the Good News of Your Son, and let me
tell of Your love and of Your grace. Make me
a faithful servant for You, Father, now and forever.
Amen

Optimism

My cup runs over. Surely goodness and mercy
shall follow me all the days of my life;
and I will dwell in the house of the Lord Forever.

Psalm 23:5, 6 NKJV

But if we look forward to something we don't have yet,
we must wait patiently and confidently.

Romans 8:25 NLT

I can do everything through him that gives me strength.

Philippians 4:13 NIV

Be of good courage, and he shall strengthen your heart,
all ye that hope in the LORD.

Psalm 31:24 KJV

Finally brothers, whatever is true, whatever is honorable,
whatever is just, whatever is pure, whatever is lovely,
whatever is commendable—if there is any moral excellence
and if there is any praise—dwell on these things.

Philippians 4:8 HCSB

C hristians have every reason to be optimistic about life. As Billy Graham observed, "Christ can put a spring in your step and a thrill in your heart. Optimism and cheerfulness are products of knowing Christ." But sometimes, when we are tired or frustrated, optimism and cheerfulness seem like distant promises. They are not. Thankfully, our God makes this promise: "I will give you a new heart and put a new spirit in you . . . ." (Ezekiel 36:26 NIV). Our task is to let Him.

Today, accept the new spirit that God seeks to infuse into your heart. Think optimistically about yourself, your students, your school, and your world. Rejoice in this glorious day that the Lord has given you, and share your optimism with your friends, with your coworkers, and with your students. Your enthusiasm will be contagious. And your words will bring healing and comfort to a world that needs both.

If you can't tell whether your glass is half-empty or half-full, you don't need another glass; what you need is better eyesight . . . and a more thankful heart.

Marie T. Freeman

— A Prayer —

Lord, give me faith, optimism, and hope. Let me expect the best from You, and let me look for the best in my students. Let me trust You, Lord, to direct my life. And, let me be Your faithful, hopeful, optimistic servant every day that I live.

Amen

Patience

*The Lord is wonderfully good to those who wait for him
and seek him. So it is good to wait quietly
for salvation from the Lord.*

Lamentations 3:25, 26 NLT

*We urge you, brethren, admonish the unruly,
encourage the fainthearted, help the weak,
be patient with everyone.*

1 Thessalonians 5:14 NASB

*It is better to be patient than powerful;
it is better to have self-control than to conquer a city.*

Proverbs 16:32 NLT

*Wherefore seeing we also are compassed about with
so great a cloud of witnesses, let us lay aside every weight,
and the sin which doth so easily beset us, and let us run
with patience the race that is set before us . . . .*

Hebrews 12:1 KJV

Your students, even the most dedicated and well-intentioned, are far from perfect. They make mistakes and misbehave; they don't always listen, and they don't always complete their assignments.

In an imperfect school filled with imperfect people, a teacher's patience is tested many times each day. But, God's instructions are clear: "be patient, bearing with one another in love" (Ephesians 4:2 NIV). And, that's as it should be. After all, think how patient God has been with us.

> Teach us, O Lord, the disciplines of patience,
> for to wait is often harder than to work.
>
> *Peter Marshall*

— A Prayer —

Dear Lord, help me to understand the wisdom of patience. When I am hurried, slow me down. When I become impatient with others, give me empathy. Today, let me be a patient servant and a patient teacher, as I serve You and bring glory to Your Son.

Amen

Peace

I leave you peace; my peace I give you.
I do not give it to you as the world does.
So don't let your hearts be troubled or afraid.

John 14:27 NCV

May the God of hope fill you with all joy and peace
as you trust in him, so that you may overflow with
hope by the power of the Holy Spirit.

Romans 15:13 NIV

And let the peace of God rule in your hearts . . .
and be ye thankful.

Colossians 3:15 KJV

You will keep in perfect peace him whose mind is steadfast,
because he trusts in you.

Isaiah 26:3 NIV

I have told you these things, so that in me
you may have peace. In this world you will have trouble.
But take heart! I have overcome the world.

John 16:33 NIV

As every teacher knows, peace can be a scarce commodity in a demanding, 21st-century classroom. How, then, can we find the peace that we so desperately desire? By turning our days and our lives over to God.

Jesus offers us peace, not as the world gives, but as He alone gives. We, as believers, can accept His peace or ignore it. When we accept God's peace, we are blessed; when we ignore it, we suffer bitter consequences.

Today, as a gift to yourself, to your family, and to your students, claim the inner peace that is your spiritual birthright: the peace of Jesus Christ. It is offered freely; it has been paid for in full; it is yours for the asking. So ask. And then share.

His peace is a direct gift through
the personal presence of the Holy Ghost.
Oswald Chambers

— A Prayer —

The world talks about peace, but only You, Lord,
can give a perfect and lasting peace. True peace comes
through the Prince of Peace, and sometimes His peace
passes all understanding. Help me to accept His peace—
and share it—this day and forever.

Amen

Persistence

Rejoice in hope; be patient in affliction;
be persistent in prayer.

Romans 12:12 HCSB

Even though good people may be bothered by trouble
seven times, they are never defeated.

Proverbs 24:16 NCV

Let us not become weary in doing good,
for at the proper time we will reap
a harvest if we do not give up.

Galatians 6:9 NIV

You need to persevere so that when you have done
the will of God, you will receive what he has promised.

Hebrews 10:36 NIV

I have fought a good fight, I have finished my course,
I have kept the faith.

2 Timothy 4:7 KJV

The familiar saying is true: "Life is a marathon, not a sprint." And, the same can be said of the teaching profession. Teaching requires perseverance, especially on those difficult days when the students are in an uproar and the lesson plan is in disarray. But, our Savior, Christ Jesus, finished what He began, and so must we.

Sometimes, God answers our prayers with silence, and when He does, we must patiently persevere. In times of trouble, we must seek God through prayer and lean upon His strength. Whatever our problems, He can handle them. Our job is to keep persevering until He does.

Untold damage has been done to the cause of Christ
because some people gear up for a sprint when
they need to train for the marathon.

Bill Hybels

— A Prayer —

Lord, when life is difficult, I am tempted to abandon
hope in the future. But You are my God, and I can draw
strength from You. Let me trust You, Father, in good
times and in bad times. Let me persevere—
even if my soul is troubled—and let me follow Your Son
Jesus Christ this day and forever.

Amen

Praise

*It is good to give thanks to the Lord, to sing praises to
the Most High. It is good to proclaim your unfailing love
in the morning, your faithfulness in the evening.*

Psalm 92:1, 2 NLT

*But as for me, I will always have hope;
I will praise you more and more.*

Psalm 71:14 NIV

*The LORD is my strength and song, and He has become
my salvation; He is my God, and I will praise Him.*

Exodus 15:2 NIV

*Through Him then, let us continually offer up
a sacrifice of praise to God, that is,
the fruit of lips that give thanks to His name.*

Hebrews 13:15 NASB

Is anyone happy? Let him sing songs of praise.

James 5:13 NIV

The Bible makes it clear: it pays to praise God. But sometimes, we allow ourselves to become so preoccupied with the demands of everyday life that we forget to say "Thank You" to the Giver of all good gifts.

Worship and praise should be a part of everything we do. Otherwise, we quickly lose perspective as we fall prey to the demands of the moment.

Do you sincerely desire to be a worthy servant of the One who has given you eternal love and eternal life? Then praise Him for who He is and for what He has done for you. And don't just praise Him on Sunday morning. Praise Him all day long, every day, for as long as you live . . . and then for all eternity.

> How delightful a teacher, but gentle a provider,
> how bountiful a giver is my Father!
> Praise, praise to Thee, O manifested Most High.
>
> *Jim Elliot*

— A Prayer —

Heavenly Father, today and every day I will praise You. I come to You with hope in my heart and words of thanksgiving on my lips. Let me follow in Christ's footsteps, and let my thoughts, my prayers, my words, and my deeds praise You now and forever.

Amen

Prayer

Let my prayer come before You; incline Your ear to my cry!
Psalm 88:2 NASB

Don't fret or worry, Instead of worrying, pray.
Let petitions and praises shape your worries into prayers,
letting God know your concerns. Before you know it,
a sense of God's wholeness, everything coming together
for good, will come and settle you down.
It's wonderful what happens when Christ displaces
worry at the center of your life.
Philippians 4:6, 7 MSG

Rejoice evermore. Pray without ceasing.
In every thing give thanks: for this is the will
of God in Christ Jesus concerning you.
1 Thessalonians 5:16-18 KJV

The effective prayer of a righteous man
can accomplish much.
James 5:16 NASB

Whatever you ask for in prayer,
believe that you have received it, and it will be yours.
Mark 11:24 NIV

Is prayer an integral part of your daily life or is it a hit-or-miss habit? Do you "pray without ceasing," or is your prayer life an afterthought? Do you regularly pray in the solitude of the early morning darkness, or do you bow your head only when others are watching?

The quality of your spiritual life will be in direct proportion to the quality of your prayer life. Prayer changes things, and it changes you. Today, instead of turning things over in your mind, turn them over to God in prayer. Instead of worrying about your next decision, ask God to lead the way. Don't limit your prayers to meals or to bedtime. Pray constantly about things great and small. God is listening, and He wants to hear from you.

He who kneels most stands best.

D. L. Moody

— A Prayer —

Dear Lord, I will open my heart to You. I will take my concerns, my fears, my plans, and my hopes to You in prayer. And, then, I will trust the answers that You give. You are my loving Father, and I will accept Your will for my life today and every day that I live.

Amen

Problems

Let not your heart be troubled:
ye believe in God, believe also in me.

John 14:1 KJV

People who do what is right may have many problems,
but the Lord will solve them all.

Psalm 34:19 NCV

Be of good cheer; I have overcome the world.

John 16:33 KJV

For though a righteous man falls seven times,
he rises again . . . .

Proverbs 24:16 NIV

Are you tired? Worn out? Burned out on religion?
Come to me. Get away with me and you'll recover your life.
I'll show you how to take a real rest. Walk with me and work
with me . . . watch how I do it. Learn the unforced rhythms
of grace. I won't lay anything heavy or ill-fitting on you.
Keep company with me and you'll learn
to live freely and lightly.

Matthew 11:28-30 MSG

American clergyman Edward Everett Hale observed, "Some people bear three kinds of trouble—the ones they've had, the ones they have, and the ones they expect to have." How true. But a better strategy for you is this: accept the past, live in the present, and place the future in God's capable hands.

As you face the challenges of everyday life—whether inside the classroom or outside it—you may be comforted by this fact: Trouble, of every kind, is temporary. Yet God's grace is eternal. And worries, of every kind, are temporary. But God's love is everlasting. The troubles that concern you will pass. God remains. And with these thoughts in mind, it's now time for you to place today's troubles in their proper perspective.

I choose joy. I will refuse the temptation to be cynical;
cynicism is the tool of a lazy thinker. I will refuse
to see people as anything less than human beings,
created by God. I will refuse to see any problem
as anything less than an opportunity to see God.

Max Lucado

— A Prayer —

Lord, sometimes my problems are simply too big for me,
but they are never too big for You.
Let me turn my troubles over to You, Lord,
and let me trust in You today and for all eternity.

Amen

Responsibility

Yet they will be rewarded individually,
according to their own hard work.

1 Corinthians 3:8 NLT

Therefore I will judge you . . .
each according to his conduct, declares the Lord GOD.

Ezekiel 18:30 NASB

Even a child is known by his actions,
by whether his conduct is pure and right.

Proverbs 20:11 NIV

And you shall do what is good and right in
the sight of the Lord, that it may be well with you . . . .

Deuteronomy 6:18 NASB

I the LORD search the heart and examine the mind,
to reward a man according to his conduct,
according to what his deeds deserve.

Jeremiah 17:10 NIV

As teachers, we find ourselves preaching the gospel of responsible behavior. Unfortunately, our sermons often fall upon deaf ears. Despite warnings to the contrary, young people sometimes behave inappropriately; they sometimes behave impulsively; they sometimes behave foolishly. Why? Because they are human beings and because they are young. Our task, as adults, is to never give up, but instead to keep teaching the wisdom of responsible behavior by word and by example. And the greatest of these, of course, is example.

Transformation will begin in any life—in yours—when you stand up and say: "I'm responsible for the kind of person I am. I am what I've wanted to be. Now I've changed my mind. I'm sorry for what I am and for what I have done. I'm going to be different. God help me."

E. Stanley Jones

—A Prayer—

Lord, my students are both a priceless gift
and a profound responsibility. Let my actions be worthy
of that responsibility. Lead me along Your path, Lord,
and guide me far from the frustrations and distractions
of this troubled world. Let Your Holy Word guide
my actions, and let Your love reside in my heart,
this day and every day.
Amen

Satisfaction

*For You, O God, have tested us; You have refined us as
silver is refined. You brought us into the net;
You laid affliction on our backs. You have caused men to ride
over our heads; we went through fire and through water;
but You brought us out to rich fulfillment.*

Psalm 66:10-12 NKJV

*Satisfy us in the morning with your unfailing love,
that we may sing for joy and be glad all our days.*

Psalm 90:14 NIV

*But godliness with contentment is great gain.
For we brought nothing into the world, and we can take
nothing out of it. But if we have food and clothing,
we will be content with that.*

1 Timothy 6:6-8 NIV

*Keep your lives free from the love of money and be content
with what you have, because God has said,
"Never will I leave you; never will I forsake you."*

Hebrews 13:5 NIV

The preoccupation with happiness and contentment is an ever-present theme in the modern world. We are bombarded with messages that tell us where to find peace and pleasure in a world that worships materialism and wealth. But, lasting satisfaction is not found in material possessions; genuine contentment is a spiritual gift from God to those who trust in Him and follow His commandments.

Where do we find contentment? If we don't find it in God, we will never find it anywhere else. But, if we put our faith and our trust in Him, we will be blessed with an inner peace that is beyond human understanding. When God dwells at the center of our lives, peace and contentment will belong to us just as surely as we belong to God.

As I contemplate all the sacrifices required in order to live a life that is totally focused on Jesus Christ and His eternal kingdom, the joy seeps out of my heart onto my face in a smile of deep satisfaction.

Anne Graham Lotz

— A Prayer —

Heavenly Father, You are my contentment and my peace. I find protection when I seek Your healing hand; I discover joy when I welcome Your healing Spirit. Let me look to You, Lord, for the peace that You have offered me through the gift of Your Son.

Amen

Seeking God

I sought the Lord, and He heard me,
and delivered me from all my fears.

Psalm 34:4 NKJV

Seek the LORD and His strength; seek His face continually.

Psalm 105:4 NASB

If my people, which are called by my name,
shall humble themselves, and pray, and seek my face,
and turn from their wicked ways; then will I hear from
heaven, and will forgive their sin, and will heal their land.

1 Chronicles 7:14 KJV

Anyone who comes to him [God] must believe that
he exists and that he rewards those who earnestly seek him.

Hebrews 11:6 NIV

Sow for yourselves righteousness, reap the fruit of unfailing
love, and break up your unplowed ground;
for it is time to seek the LORD, until he comes
and showers righteousness on you.

Hosea 10:12 NIV

Where is God? He is everywhere you have ever been and everywhere you will ever go. He is with you throughout the night and all through the day; He knows your every thought; He hears your every heartbeat.

When you earnestly seek Him, you will find Him because He is here, waiting patiently for you to reach out to Him . . . right here . . . right now. And make no mistake: your soul does indeed thirst for God. That thirst that is planted in your heart, and it is a thirst that only God can quench. Let Him . . . right here . . . right now.

Seeking after God is a two-pronged endeavor.
It requires not only humility to say, "God, I need you,"
but also a heart that desires a pure life
that is pleasing to the Lord.

Jim Cymbala

— A Prayer —

Dear Lord, You promise that if I seek You, I will find
You. You are with me, Father, every step that I take.
Let me reach out to You, and let me praise You
for revealing Your Word, Your way, and Your love.
Amen

Self-Discipline

*So prepare your minds for service and have self-control.
All your hope should be for the gift of grace that will be
yours when Jesus Christ is shown to you.*

1 Peter 1:13 NCV

*My son, do not despise the Lord's discipline and do not
resent his rebuke, because the Lord disciplines those he loves,
as a father the son he delights in.*

Proverbs 3:11, 12 NIV

Folly is loud; she is undisciplined and without knowledge.

Proverbs 9:13 NIV

*Whoever gives heed to instruction prospers,
and blessed is he that trusts in the Lord.*

Proverbs 16:20 NIV

*No discipline seems pleasant at the time, but painful.
Later on, however, it produces a harvest of righteousness
and peace for those who have been trained by it.*

Hebrews 12:11 NIV

As leaders of the classroom, we are charged with teaching discipline and, on occasion, dispensing it. We do so in the hopes that our students will learn that disciplined behavior is at the very foundation of successful living.

Those who study the Bible are confronted again and again with God's intention that His children (of all ages) lead disciplined lives. God doesn't reward laziness or misbehavior. To the contrary, He expects His own to adopt a disciplined approach to their lives, and He punishes those who disobey His commandments.

Wise teachers demonstrate the importance of self-discipline by their words and by their actions. Wise students pay attention . . . and learn.

Simply stated, self-discipline is obedience to God's Word and willingness to submit everything in life to His will, for His ultimate glory.

John MacArthur

— A Prayer —

Heavenly Father, make me a teacher of discipline and righteousness, and make me a diligent teacher in the service of Your Son, Christ Jesus. Let me teach others by the faithfulness of my conduct, and let me follow Your will and Your Word, today and every day.

Amen

Serving God

Be strong and of good courage, and do it;
do not fear nor be dismayed, for the Lord God—my God—
will be with you. He will not leave you nor forsake you,
until you have finished all the work for
the service of the house of the Lord.

1 Chronicles 28:20 NKJV

Exercise your freedom by serving God,
not by breaking rules. Treat everyone you meet
with dignity. Love your spiritual family. Revere God.
Respect the government.

1 Peter 2:16, 17 MSG

Choose you this day whom ye will serve . . .
as for me and my house, we will serve the LORD.

Joshua 24:15 KJV

Therefore, I urge you, brothers, in view of God's mercy,
to offer your bodies as living sacrifices, holy and pleasing
to God—this is your spiritual act of worship.

Romans 12:1 NIV

As a teacher, you have chosen a life of service. Congratulations. When you decided to become a teacher, you demonstrated your willingness to serve your Father in heaven—and His children here on earth—in a very tangible way. As a result, you can be comforted by the knowledge that your kindness and generosity will touch the lives of students in ways that you may never fully comprehend. But God knows the impact of your good works, and He will bless you because of them.

The words of Galatians 6:9 are clear: "Let us not become weary in doing good, for at the proper time we will reap a harvest if we do not give up" (NIV). May you never grow weary of your role as a teacher, and may your good works continue to bless your students long after the final school bell has rung.

That's what I love about serving God. In His eyes, there are no little people . . . because there are no big people. We are all on the same playing field.

Joni Eareckson Tada

— A Prayer —

Dear Lord, let me serve You and follow
Your commandments. When I am tempted to stray from
Your Word and from Your will, direct my thoughts
back to You. Lead me far from temptation, Lord,
so that I might serve You and only You.
Amen

Serving Others

Be devoted to one another in brotherly love.
Honor one another above yourselves.

Romans 12:10 NIV

The one who blesses others is abundantly blessed;
those who help others are helped.

Proverbs 11:25 MSG

But whosoever will be great among you,
let him be your minister; and whosoever will be chief among
you, let him be your servant: even as the Son of man
came not to be ministered unto, but to minister,
and to give his life a ransom for many.

Matthew 20:26-28 KJV

The greatest among you will be your servant.
For whoever exalts himself will be humbled,
and whoever humbles himself will be exalted.

Matthew 23:11 NIV

Each of you should look not only to your own interests,
but also to the interest of others.

Philippians 2:4 NIV

The teachings of Jesus are clear: We achieve greatness through service to others. And, as teachers, we have unique and important opportunities for service. Each time we pause to help a student, each time we offer a kind word or a pat on the back, we have done so in accordance with the commandments of our Savior. If we seek spiritual greatness, we must first become servants. Then, and only then, will we achieve greatness in the eyes of our Lord.

I have discovered that when I please Christ,
I end up inadvertently serving others
far more effectively.

Beth Moore

— A Prayer —

Dear Lord, give me a servant's heart.
When Jesus humbled Himself and became a servant,
He also became an example for His followers.
Make me a faithful steward of my gifts,
and let me share with those in need.
Amen

Strength

God is our refuge and strength,
a very present help in trouble.

Psalm 46:1 NKJV

Come to Me, all you who are weary and burdened,
and I will give you rest. Take My yoke upon you and
learn from Me, because I am gentle and humble in heart,
and you will find rest for your souls.
For My yoke is easy and My burden is light.

Matthew 11:28-30 HCSB

Those who hope in the LORD will renew their strength.
They will soar on wings like eagles;
they will run and not grow weary,
they will walk and not be faint.

Isaiah 40:31 NIV

He said unto me, My grace is sufficient for thee:
for my strength is made perfect in weakness.

2 Corinthians 12:9 KJV

I can do all things through Him who strengthens me.

Philippians 4:13 NASB

If you're a teacher with too many obligations and too few hours in which to meet them, you are not alone: yours is a demanding profession. As a dedicated teacher, you may experience moments when you feel overworked, overstressed, and under-appreciated. Thankfully, God stands ready to renew your optimism and your strength if you turn to Him.

When you feel worried or weary, focus your thoughts upon God and upon His love for you. Then, ask Him for the wisdom to prioritize your life and the strength to fulfill your responsibilities. God will give you the energy to do the most important things on today's to-do list . . . if you ask Him. So ask Him.

When God is our strength, it is strength indeed;
when our strength is our own, it is only weakness.

St. Augustine

— A Prayer —

Lord, sometimes life is difficult. Sometimes, my students worry me, weary me, or break my heart. But, when I lift my eyes to You, Father, You strengthen me. Lord, You are my strength, my hope, and my salvation.
Amen

Success

And may the Lord our God show us his approval
and make our efforts successful.
Yes, make our efforts successful!

Psalm 90:17 NLT

Blessed in the man who does not walk in the counsel of
the wicked or stand in the way of sinners or sit in
the seat of mockers. But his delight is in the law
of the LORD, and on his law he meditates day and night.
He is like a tree planted by streams of water,
which yields its fruit in season and whose leaf
does not wither. Whatever he does prospers.

Psalm 1:1-3 NIV

Commit to the Lord whatever you do,
· and your plans will succeed.

Proverbs 16:3 NIV

You need to persevere so that when you have done
the will of God, you will receive what he has promised.

Hebrews 10:36 NIV

But as for you, be strong and do not give up,
for your work will be rewarded.

2 Chronicles 15:7 NIV

How do you define success? Do you define it as the accumulation of material possessions or the adulation of your neighbors? If so, you need to reorder your priorities. Genuine success has little to do with fame or fortune; it has everything to do with God's gift of love and His promise of salvation.

If you have accepted Christ as your personal savior, you are already a towering success in the eyes of God, but there is still more that you can do. Your task—as a believer who has been touched by the Creator's grace—is to accept the spiritual abundance and peace that He offers through the person of His Son. Then, you can share the healing message of God's love and His abundance with a world that desperately needs both. When you do, you have reached the pinnacle of success.

> Success or failure can be pretty well predicted
> by the degree to which the heart is fully in it.
> *John Eldredge*

— A Prayer —

Dear Lord, let Your priorities be my priorities.
Let Your will be my will. Let Your Word be my guide,
and keep me mindful that genuine success is a result,
not of the world's approval, but of *Your* approval.
Amen

Talents

Each man has his own gift from God;
one has this gift, another has that.

1 Corinthians 7:7 NIV

I remind you to fan into flame the gift of God.

2 Timothy 1:6 NIV

Thanks be to God for his indescribable gift!

2 Corinthians 9:15 NIV

We have different gifts, according to the grace given us.
If a man's gift is prophesying, let him use it
in proportion to his faith. If it is serving, let him serve;
if it is teaching, let him teach; if it is encouraging,
let him encourage; if it is contributing to the needs of others,
let him give generously; if it is leadership,
let him govern diligently; if it is showing mercy,
let him do it cheerfully.

Romans 12:6-8 NIV

Every day of your life, you have a choice to make: nurture your talents or neglect them. When you choose wisely, God rewards your efforts, and He expands your opportunities to serve Him.

We live in a world in which leisure is glorified and misbehavior is glamorized. But God has other plans. He did not create us for lives of mischief or mediocrity; He created us for far greater things. He created us with the intention that we use our talents for His glory.

How will you use God's gifts today? If you are wise, you will seek fresh opportunities to fan your own spark of talent into a roaring flame.

In the great orchestra we call life, you have
an instrument and a song, and you owe it to God
to play them both sublimely.

Max Lucado

— A Prayer —

Lord, You have given all of us talents, and I am
no exception. You have blessed me with the talent of
teaching—let me nurture it, and use it to the glory of
Your Kingdom. Today, let me be a good and faithful
steward, Father, of my talents and my possessions.
Let me share my gifts with my students, and let me offer
praise to You, the Giver of all things good.

Amen

Teaching

*Refuse to get involved in inane discussions; they always end
up in fights. God's servant must not be argumentative,
but a gentle listener and a teacher who keeps cool,
working firmly but patiently with those who refuse to obey.*

2 Timothy 2:23, 24 MSG

*He will teach us His ways,
and we shall walk in His paths.*

Isaiah 2:3 NKJV

*A wise man's heart guides his mouth,
and his lips promote instruction.*

Proverbs 16:23 NIV

*Whoever gives heed to instruction prospers,
and blessed is he that trusts in the Lord.*

Proverbs 16:20 NIV

*A wise person gets known for insight;
gracious words add to one's reputation.
True intelligence is a spring of fresh water,
while fools sweat it out the hard way.*

Proverbs 16:21, 22 MSG

Daniel Webster wrote, "If we work in marble, it will perish; if we work upon brass, time will efface it; if we rear temples, they will crumble into dust; but if we work upon immortal minds and instill in them just principles, we are then engraving upon tablets which no time will efface, but which will brighten and brighten to all eternity." These words remind us of the glorious opportunities that are available to those of us who teach. May we, with God's help, touch the hearts and minds of our students and, in doing so, refashion this wonderful world . . . and the next.

If you want to be a teacher, remember
that you're just as likely to teach who you are
as you are to teach what you know.

Marie T. Freeman

— A Prayer —

Dear Lord, make me a worthy teacher, a humble servant,
and a faithful disciple of Your Son Jesus. Let me guide
my students in the way that You would have them go,
and let me be an example of righteousness
and faithfulness today and every day.
Amen

Thanksgiving

And let the peace of God rule in your hearts . . .
and be ye thankful.

Colossians 3:15 KJV

In everything give thanks;
for this is the will of God in Christ Jesus for you.

1 Thessalonians 5:18 NKJV

O come, let us sing unto the LORD:
let us make a joyful noise to the rock of our salvation.
Let us come before his presence with thanksgiving,
and make a joyful noise unto him with psalms.

Psalm 95:1, 2 KJV

I know that the righteous personally thank you,
that good people are secure in your presence.

Psalm 140:13 MSG

Do you see what we've got? An unshakable kingdom!
And do you see how thankful we must be?
Not only thankful, but brimming with worship,
deeply reverent before God.

Hebrews 12:27, 28 MSG

As Christians, we are blessed beyond measure. And, as teachers, we are especially blessed by the opportunity to educate young minds and shape young lives. Of course we should be grateful, but as busy professionals caught between the rush of everyday living and the demands of the classroom, we may forget to offer thanks to God for His countless blessings.

When we slow down and express our gratitude to our Creator, we enrich our own lives and the lives of those around us. Thanksgiving should become a habit, a regular part of our daily routines. Yes, God has blessed us beyond measure, and we owe Him everything, including our eternal praise.

Thanksgiving or complaining—these words express two contrastive attitudes of the souls of God's children in regard to His dealings with them. The soul that gives thanks can find comfort in everything; the soul that complains can find comfort in nothing.

Hannah Whitall Smith

— A Prayer —

Dear Lord, sometimes, amid the demands of the day, I lose perspective, and I fail to give thanks for Your blessings and for Your love. Today, help me to count those blessings, and let me give thanks to You, Father, for Your love, for Your grace, for Your blessings, and for Your Son.

Amen

Thoughts

Those who are pure in their thinking are happy,
because they will be with God.

Matthew 5:8 NCV

Set your mind on the things above,
not on the things that are on earth.

Colossians 3:2 NASB

Commit your works to the Lord,
and your thoughts will be established.

Proverbs 16:3 NKJV

May the words of my mouth and the thoughts of
my heart be pleasing to you, O LORD,
my rock and my redeemer.

Psalm 19:14 NLT

Do not conform any longer to the pattern of this world,
but be transformed by the renewing of your mind.
Then you will be able to test and approve what
God's will is—his good, pleasing and perfect will.

Romans 12:2 NIV

Because we are human, we are always busy with our thoughts. We simply can't help ourselves. Our brains never shut off, and even while we're sleeping, we mull things over in our minds. The question is not if we will think; the question is how will we think and what will we think about.

Today, focus your thoughts on God and His will. And if you've been plagued by pessimism and doubt, stop thinking like that! Place your faith in God and give thanks for His blessings. Think optimistically about your world and your life. It's the wise way to use your mind. And besides, since you will always be busy with your thoughts, you might as well make those thoughts pleasing (to God) and helpful (to you and yours).

> It is the thoughts and intents of the heart
> that shape a person's life.
>
> *John Eldredge*

— A Prayer —

Dear Lord, keep my thoughts focused on Your love,
Your power, Your promises, and Your Son.
When I am worried, I will turn to You for comfort; when
I am weak, I will turn to You for strength; when I am
troubled, I will turn to You for patience and perspective.
Help me guard my thoughts, Father, so that I may
honor You today and every day that I live.
Amen

Today

For he says, "In the time of my favor I heard you,
and in the day of salvation I helped you."
I tell you, now is the time of God's favor,
now is the day of salvation.

2 Corinthians 6:2 NIV

This is the day the LORD has made;
let us rejoice and be glad in it.

Psalm 118:24 NIV

Encourage one another daily, as long as it is Today . . . .

Hebrews 3:13 NIV

Give your entire attention to what God is doing right now,
and don't get worked up about what
may or may not happen tomorrow.
God will help you deal with whatever
hard things come up when the time comes.

Matthew 6:33, 34 MSG

For Christian believers, every day begins and ends with God and His Son. Christ came to this earth to give us abundant life and eternal salvation. Our task is to accept Christ's grace with joy in our hearts and praise on our lips. Believers who fashion their days around Jesus are transformed: They see the world differently, they act differently, and they feel differently about themselves and their neighbors.

The familiar words of Psalm 118:24 remind us that every day is a gift from God. So whatever this day holds for you, begin it and end it with God as your partner and Christ as your Savior. And throughout the day, give thanks to the One who created you and saved you. God's love for you is infinite. Accept it joyously and be thankful.

Today is mine. Tomorrow is none of my business.
If I peer anxiously into the fog of the future,
I will strain my spiritual eyes so that I will not see
clearly what is required of me now.

Elisabeth Elliot

— A Prayer —

This is the day that You have given me, Lord. Let me
be thankful, and let me use it according to Your plan.
I praise You, Father, for the gift of life and for the
friends, the family members, and the students who make
my life rich. Enable me to live each moment to
the fullest, totally involved in Your will.

Amen

Trusting God

*The Good News shows how God makes people right
with himself—that it begins and ends with faith.
As the Scripture says, "But those who are right with God will
live by trusting in him."*

Romans 1:17 NCV

*For the Lord God is our light and our protector.
He gives us grace and glory. No good thing will the Lord
withhold from those who do what is right. O Lord Almighty,
happy are those who trust in you.*

Psalm 84:11, 12 NLT

*Trust ye in the LORD for ever:
for in the LORD JEHOVAH is everlasting strength.*

Isaiah 26:4 KJV

*But it is good for me to draw near to God:
I have put my trust in the Lord GOD.*

Psalm 73:28 KJV

*Do not let your hearts be troubled. Trust in God;
trust also in me. In my Father's house are many rooms;
if it were not so, I would have told you.
I am going there to prepare a place for you.*

John 14:1, 2 NIV

Do you aspire to do great things for God's kingdom? Then trust Him. Trust Him with every aspect of your life. Trust Him with your relationships. Trust Him with your finances. Trust Him with your profession. Follow His commandments and pray for His guidance. Then, wait patiently for God's revelations and for His blessings. In His own fashion and in His own time, God will bless you in ways that you never could have imagined.

When we are in a situation where Jesus is all we have,
we soon discover he is all we really need.
Gigi Graham Tchividjian

— A Prayer —

Dear Lord, even when I don't understand
why things happen, I will trust You.
Even when I am confused or worried, I will trust You.
There are many things that I cannot do, Lord,
and there are many things that I cannot understand.
But one thing I can do is to trust You always.
And I will.
Amen

Wisdom

The fear of the Lord is the beginning of wisdom;
a good understanding have all those who do
His commandments. His praise endures forever.

Psalm 111:10 NKJV

Choose my instruction instead of silver, knowledge rather
than choice gold, for wisdom is more precious than rubies,
and nothing you desire can compare with her.

Proverbs 8:10, 11 NIV

Do not deceive yourselves. If any one of you thinks he is
wise by the standards of this age,
he should become a "fool" so that he may become wise.
For the wisdom of this world is foolishness in God's sight.

1 Corinthians 3:18, 19 NIV

But if any of you lacks wisdom, let him ask of God,
who gives to all generously and without reproach,
and it will be given to him.

James 1:5 NASB

I will instruct you and teach you in the way you should go;
I will counsel you and watch over you.

Psalm 32:8 NIV

Wisdom is not accumulated overnight. It is like a savings account that accrues slowly over time, and the person who consistently adds to his account will eventually accumulate a great sum. The secret to success is consistency. Do you seek wisdom for yourself and for your students? Then keep learning and keep motivating them to do likewise. The ultimate source of wisdom, of course, is—first and foremost—the Word of God. When you begin a daily study of God's Word and live according to His commandments, you will become wise . . . and so, in time, will your students.

Wise people listen to wise instruction,
especially instruction from the Word of God.

Warren Wiersbe

— A Prayer —

Lord, make me a teacher of wisdom and discernment.
Lead me in Your ways and teach me from Your Word
so that, in time, my wisdom might glorify
Your Kingdom and Your Son.

Amen

Words

How forcible are right words!

Job 6:25 KJV

For out of the overflow of the heart the mouth speaks.

Matthew 12:34 NIV

To everything there is a season . . .
a time to keep silence, and a time to speak.

Ecclesiastes 3:1, 7 KJV

But I say unto you, That every idle word that men shall
speak, they shall give account thereof in the day of judgment.
For by thy words thou shalt be justified,
and by thy words thou shalt be condemned.

Matthew 12:36, 37 KJV

Let the words of my mouth, and the meditations of my heart,
be acceptable in thy sight, O Lord,
my strength and my redeemer.

Psalm 19:14 KJV

The Bible reminds us that "Reckless words pierce like a sword, but the tongue of the wise brings healing" (Proverbs 12:18 NIV). In other words, if we are to solve more problems than we start, we must measure our words carefully.

Sometimes, even the most thoughtful teachers may speak first and think second (with decidedly mixed results). A far better strategy, of course, is to do the more difficult thing: to think first and to speak next.

Do you seek to be a source of encouragement to your students? If so, you must speak words that are worthy of your Savior. Avoid angry outbursts. Refrain from impulsive outpourings. Terminate tantrums. Instead, speak words of encouragement and hope to a world that desperately needs both.

> Words. Do you fully understand their power?
> Can any of us really grasp the mighty force
> behind the things we say? Do we stop and
> think before we speak, considering
> the potency of the words we utter?
>
> *Joni Eareckson Tada*

— A Prayer —

Dear Lord, You have commanded me to choose
my words carefully so that I might be a source of
encouragement to my students. Keep me mindful,
Lord, of the influence I have on many people.
Let the words that I speak today be worthy of
the One who has saved me forever.
Amen

Work

. . . and each one will receive his own reward
according to his own labor.

1 Corinthians 3:8 NKJV

Work hard so God can approve you. Be a good worker,
one who does not need to be ashamed
and who correctly explains the word of truth.

2 Timothy 2:15 NLT

But let every man prove his own work,
and then shall he have rejoicing in himself alone,
and not in another.
For every man shall bear his own burden.

Galatians 6:4, 5 KJV

Be strong and courageous, and do the work.
Do not be afraid or discouraged,
for the Lord God, my God, is with you.

1 Chronicles 28:20 NIV

But as for you, be strong and do not give up,
for your work will be rewarded.

2 Chronicles 15:7 NIV

Being a teacher is not only a rewarding profession, it's also a demanding one. The pressures of the classroom, combined with late-night paper-grading marathons and lesson preparations, can leave even the most experienced teachers feeling overworked and under-appreciated.

Because of your profession, you have countless opportunities to accomplish great things for God—but you should *not* expect the work to be easy. Reaching for greatness usually requires lots of effort, which is perfectly fine with Your Heavenly Father. After all, He knows that you're up to the task, and He has big plans for you *and* for your students. Very big plans . . .

So let us lift up our work as a sacrifice, acceptable
because it is lifted up to him who alone can purify.
Elisabeth Elliot

— A Prayer —

Dear Lord, make my work pleasing to You.
Help me to sow the seeds of Your abundance
in the classroom and everywhere I go.
Let me be diligent in all my undertakings
and give me patience to wait for Your harvest.
Amen

Worship

God lifted him high and honored him far beyond anyone or
anything, ever, so that all created beings in heaven and earth,
even those long ago dead and buried, will bow in worship
before this Jesus Christ, and call out in praise that he is
the Master of all, to the glorious honor of God the Father.

Philippians 2:9, 11 MSG

Worship the Lord with gladness. Come before him,
singing with joy. Acknowledge that the Lord is God!
He made us, and we are his.
We are his people, the sheep of his pasture.

Psalm 100:2, 3 NLT

Happy are those who hear the joyful call to worship,
for they will walk in the light of your presence, Lord.

Psalm 89:15 NLT

I was glad when they said unto me,
Let us go into the house of the LORD.

Psalm 122:1 KJV

God has a wonderful plan for your life, and an important part of that plan includes worship. We should never deceive ourselves: Every life is based upon some form of worship. The question is not *whether* we worship, but *what* we worship.

Have you accepted the grace of God's only begotten Son? Then worship Him. Worship Him today and every day. Worship Him with sincerity and thanksgiving. Write His name on your heart and rest assured that He, too, has written your name on His.

It's the definition of worship: A hungry heart finding
the Father's feast. A searching soul finding
the Father's face. A wandering pilgrim spotting
the Father's house. Finding God. Finding God
seeking us. This is worship. This is a worshiper.

Max Lucado

— A Prayer —

When I worship You, Lord, You direct my path and You cleanse my heart. Let today and every day be a time of worship and praise. Let me worship You in everything that I think and do. Thank You, Lord, for the priceless gift of Your Son Jesus. Let me be worthy of that gift, and let me give You the praise and the glory forever.

Amen